Blueprints for EAP 1640

Miami Dade College

Keith S. Folse | M. Kathleen Mahnke | Elena Vestri Solomon
| Lorraine Williams

CENGAGE
Learning·

Australia • Brazil • Japan • Korea • Mexico • Singapore • Spain • United Kingdom • United States

Blueprints for EAP 1640: Miami Dade College

Blueprints 2: Composition and Grammar Skills for Academic Writing
M. Kathleen Mahnke, Elena Vestri Solomon, Lorraine Williams Lorraine Williams

Senior Project Development Manager:
 Linda deStefano

Market Development Manager:
 Heather Kramer

Senior Production/Manufacturing Manager:
 Donna M. Brown

Production Editorial Manager:
 Kim Fry

Sr. Rights Acquisition Account Manager:
 Todd Osborne

For product information and technology assistance, contact us at
Cengage Learning Customer & Sales Support, 1-800-354-9706

For permission to use material from this text or product,
submit all requests online at **cengage.com/permissions**
Further permissions questions can be emailed to
permissionrequest@cengage.com

This book contains select works from existing Cengage Learning resources and was produced by Cengage Learning Custom Solutions for collegiate use. As such, those adopting and/or contributing to this work are responsible for editorial content accuracy, continuity and completeness.

Compilation © 2013 Cengage Learning
ISBN-13: 978-1-285-90620-1

ISBN-10: 1-285-90620-9

Cengage Learning
5191 Natorp Boulevard
Mason, Ohio 45040
USA

Cengage Learning is a leading provider of customized learning solutions with office locations around the globe, including Singapore, the United Kingdom, Australia, Mexico, Brazil, and Japan. Locate your local office at:
international.cengage.com/region.
Cengage Learning products are represented in Canada by Nelson Education, Ltd.
For your lifelong learning solutions, visit **www.cengage.com/custom.**
Visit our corporate website at **www.cengage.com.**

Printed in the United States of America

Blueprints 2

CONTENTS

Unit 1
PARAGRAPH TO ESSAY   1

Unit 5
CAUSE/EFFECT ESSAYS   117

Unit 6
REACTION ESSAYS   144

Unit 7
ARGUMENTATIVE ESSAYS   167

Unit 8
PARAPHRASING, SUMMARIZING, AND SYNTHESIZING IN ACADEMIC WRITING   200

BLUEPRINTS 2 SKILLS CHART (PART A)

Unit	Blueprint Topics	Coherence Devices/ Transition Expressions	Grammar Focus and Sentence Check	Skills Practice
1 Paragraph to Essay	The Paragraph Unity and Coherence in Paragraphs The Essay The Thesis Statement Essay Introductions The Body of the Essay Essay Conclusions			Reviewing paragraph structure Working with essay introductions, bodies, and conclusions Incorporating unity and coherence in writing
2 Classification Essays	What Is a Classification Essay? Unity in Classification Essays Coherence in Classification Essays	one/another/a third (fourth, etc.) + classifying word	Passive voice Adjective clauses	Determining principles of classification Classifying information Maintaining unity and coherence in classification essays
3 Process Essays	What is a Process Essay? Types of Process Essays Introductions in Process Essays Conclusions in Process Essays Unity in Process Essays Coherence in Process Essays	first (second, third, etc.), next, now, then, finally, before, after, once, as soon as, while + sentence; during, over, between + noun phrase	Articles Adverb clauses	Understanding analytical and informational processess Thinking about your audience Explaining a process Maintaining unity and coherence in process essays
4 Comparison/ Contrast Essays	What is a Comparison/ Contrast Essay? Three Oraganizational Methods of Comparison/Contrast Unity in Comparison/ Contrast Essays Coherence in Comparison/ Contrast Essays	both noun and noun, not only . . . but also . . ., nevertheless, on one hand . . . on the other hand, in contrast, whereas, unlike + noun, like + noun, conversely, although, even though, though	Comparisons Parallelism	Working with different methods of organization for comparison/ contrast Maintaining unity and coherence in comparison/ contrast essays

BLUEPRINTS 2 SKILLS CHART (PART A CONTINUED)

Unit	Blueprint Topics	Coherence Devices/ Transition Expressions	Grammar Focus and Sentence Check	Skills Practice
5 Cause/Effect Essays	What is a Cause/Effect Essay? Methods of Organization for Cause/Effect Essays Unity in Cause/Effect Essays Coherence in Cause/Effect Essays	*because/as/since + s + v, therefore, consequently, thus, as a result + s + v, as a result of*	Verb tense review Fragments, run-ons, and comma splices	Working with different methods of cause/effect organization Maintaining unity and coherence in cause/effect essays
6 Reaction Essays	What is a Reaction Essay? Unity in Reaction Essays Coherence in Reaction Essays	Repeating key terms or phrases Using pronouns Using synonyms	Word forms Sentence variety	Practicing reactions Maintaining unity and coherence in reaction essays
7 Argumentative Essays	What Is an Argumentative Essay? Developing and Supporting an Argument Understanding Both Sides Maintaining a Stance Introductions in Argumentative Essays Methods of Organization for Argumentative Essays Unity in Argumentative Essays Coherence in Argumentative Essays	*although it may be true that, despite the fact that, certainly, surely*	Prepositions Noun clauses	Determining the opposing sides of an argument Working with different methods of organizing arguments Supporting arguments with details Maintaining unity and coherence in argumentative essays

BLUEPRINTS 2 SKILLS CHART (PART B) *THE WRITING PROCESS*

Unit	Prewriting	Planning	Writing	Additional Writing Assignments from the Academic Disciplines
1 Paragraph to Essay	Brainstorming	Outlining Giving and receiving feedback on outlines	Writing an essay Giving and receiving feedback on first draft Editing and revising Completing final draft	– Business – Science – Technology – Literature
2 Classification Essays	Using a questionnaire	Using a tree diagram Giving and receiving feedback on tree diagrams	Writing a classification essay, using "posing a question" as an introductory technique Giving and receiving feedback on first draft Editing and revising Completing final draft	– Business – Science – Technology – Social Science – Linguistics
3 Process Essays	Visualizing Sketching Listing	Using a flow chart Giving and receiving feedback on flowcharts	Writing a process essay, using the "funnel method" as an introductory technique Giving and receiving feedback on first draft Editing and revising	– Business – Science – Anthropology – Psychology
4 Comparison/ Contrast Essays	Listing	Using a T-diagram Giving and receiving feedback on T-diagrams	Writing a comparison/contrast essay, using "quotation" as an introductory hook Giving and receiving feedback on first draft Editing and revising Completing final draft	– Business – Science – History – Linguistics – Travel

BLUEPRINTS 2 SKILLS CHART (PART B CONTINUED) *THE WRITING PROCESS*

Unit	Prewriting	Planning	Writing	Additional Writing Assignments from the Academic Disciplines
5 Cause/Effect Essays	Using a spoke diagram	Using a chart Giving and receiving feedback on charts	Writing a cause/effect essay, using a "dramatic statement" as an introductory technique Giving and receiving feedback on first draft Editing and revising Completing final draft	– Business – Science – Technology – Geology – Current Issues
6 Reaction Essays	Using your eyes as "a camera"	Combining reactions and descriptions in a chart Giving and receiving feedback on charts	Writing a reaction essay, giving background information in the introduction Giving and receiving feedback on first draft Editing and revising Completing final draft	– Entertainment – Politics – Literature – Lecture Analysis
7 Argumentative Essays	Searching for sources of information to support your argument	Synthesizing information from outside sources Outlining	Writing an argumentative essay, using "turning an argument on its head" as an introductory technique Giving and receiving feedback on first draft Editing and revising Completing final draft	– Business – Science – Sociology/Political – Science – Linguistics

Unit 8

This section includes special instruction and practice in the important academic writing skills of paraphrasing, summarizing, and synthesizing information.

WELCOME TO BLUEPRINTS!

Blueprints 2: Composition Skills for Academic Writing is the second in a two-volume writing series for students of English as a second language. *Blueprints 2* is designed for students at the high-intermediate and advanced levels. *Blueprints 1* is designed for intermediate-level students. Both books are aimed at preparing students for success in academic writing. *Blueprints 1* focuses primarily on the paragraph, with a final unit devoted to the essay. *Blueprints 2* moves students from the paragraph to the essay in its first unit and focuses on the essay from that point on. Each *Blueprints* text features direct instruction in academic composition skills, short reading passages that serve as blueprints for writing tasks, presentations of key ESL grammar points, a large number of practice exercises, and a variety of real writing assignments.

Without a doubt, good writing requires many skills. Good writing requires your ability to use words and sentences correctly, and very good writing requires the ability to organize these words and sentences into paragraphs and essays that readers can understand well. Good writing means mastery of basic punctuation, capitalization, and spelling rules. In addition, good writing includes a solid grasp of English sentence structure, or grammar, to express ideas in writing that is accurate and appropriate.

Good writing in an academic setting often requires you to take information from one or more sources to produce a piece of writing that satisfies a certain writing task. Common examples of these academic writing tasks include summarizing a story, reacting to a piece of writing, and combining information into a new paragraph or essay.

Blueprints prepares you to be a good academic writer. One of the primary goals of the *Blueprints* books is to help you move beyond writing simple paragraphs and essays that are based on general or personal information to writing paragraphs and essays that are based on academic-level readings. The tasks in these books mirror what you will have to do in your college-level courses.

The following chart lists some special features of the *Blueprints* texts and their benefits to you.

FEATURE	BENEFIT
Blueprint readings exemplifying writing	The readings provide examples of good writing.
Grammar instruction and practice	The grammar instruction and practice help student writers master grammar in their writing.
Paraphrasing, summarizing, and synthesizing practice	These three specific skills may be the best help students will ever find for composition.
Academic writing assignments at the end of each unit	Student writing can actually reflect their learning goals.

PREFACE TO BLUEPRINTS 2

Text Organization

Blueprints 2 is divided into eight units. Unit 1 reviews the elements of a good paragraph and introduces the essay. It also introduces strategies for maintaining unity and coherence in academic writing and provides students with a variety of techniques for writing effective introductions. Concepts introduced in Unit 1 are recycled and further developed in subsequent units. Unity and coherence, for example, are revisited in each successive unit, and each successive unit also focuses on one of the introductory techniques introduced in Unit 1. Units 2 through 7 practice different kinds of essays. Unit 8 differs somewhat in format from the other units. It treats the important academic writing skills of paraphrasing, summarizing, and synthesizing.

This book is organized with a rhetorical mode as the primary vehicle for practicing organized composition. Unit 2 practices classification essays, perhaps the most straightforward of the essay types. Unit 3 focuses on process essays. Unit 4 features comparison/contrast essays. Unit 5 provides practice in cause/effect essays, and Unit 6 introduces the reaction essay. Unit 7 provides instruction and practice in the argumentative essay, one of the most common, yet most complex, essay types used in academic writing. These rhetorical modes were chosen because surveys of college and university programs cited them as those most often taught in freshman writing programs.

Contents of a Unit

Part A

Composition Lesson

Each unit begins with the core material for the unit, consisting of a presentation of the rhetorical mode for that unit. This presentation is followed by a series of short exercises that provide step-by-step practice with the unit's writing lesson.

Readings

Because of the important link between reading and writing, every unit contains two *Blueprints* reading passages (150–250 words) that students work with before they attempt any original writing. Each reading passage is designed to be a model of the rhetorical mode being taught. Each also models an introductory technique that students will practice later. All readings are preceded by a brief set of questions to help activate the schema necessary for ultimate reading comprehension. Along with each reading passage are glossed key vocabulary as well as questions that require students to analyze not only the content of the passage but also various composition elements that are featured in the reading passage. The focus on vocabulary is extremely important because a more solid grasp of lexical items will help students move from basic writing to more advanced writing. Likewise, the focus on composition elements provides not only focused instruction but also sufficient guided practice.

Grammar Focus and Sentence Check

Because grammar is such an integral part of any good writing, there are two kinds of grammar presentations in each unit: discrete grammar and sentence-level grammar. The points practiced in these two categories vary from unit to unit and are designed to address grammar that is particularly challenging for ESL writers.

Part B

Writing Assignment

Students are given a specific writing assignment that is based on the rhetorical mode presented in the unit. In Unit 4, for example, students write an original comparison/contrast essay. With all students working on the same assignment, the writing instructor has an opportunity to teach the whole group. At any point during the writing process, the teacher and class can address areas of concern.

Prewriting

Each unit presents some type of prewriting activity. This particular activity varies from unit to unit.

Planning

After generating ideas, students use a planning device or technique to organize them. Once again the details of this activity vary from unit to unit.

Partner Feedback 1

After the planning process, students are encouraged to give one another feedback. Feedback at this stage helps to identify areas that students should attend to before attempting a first draft.

First draft

As students write their first draft, they can use the special checklists for writing introductions, bodies, and conclusions that can help them produce unified and coherent essays.

Partner Feedback 2

Feedback is again encouraged after the first draft. As many academic classes require group work, repeated practice with a familiar and sympathetic ESL audience is helpful in a general way. In addition, group/pair work also allows students to exchange ideas about a given topic. Finally, group/pair work can be valuable because other student readers tend to be more critical than the writer and therefore more likely to find errors than students usually do in self-editing.

Final Draft

At this point, students are asked to revise their work again, using the feedback they received from their peers and teachers. Another checklist is provided to guide them in reviewing their work one final time.

Additional Writing Assignments from the Academic Disciplines

A unique feature of this book is a chart found at the end of every unit. This chart features a list of four to six academic areas, each with a writing prompt for a topic. The writing prompts lend themselves well to the rhetorical mode being presented and practiced in that particular unit.

Appendices

In addition to the appendix for Partner Feedback Forms, *Blueprints 2* provides appendices on Paragraph Practice, Guidelines for Partner Feedback, Creating Essay Titles, and Finding and Documenting Information from Sources.

Answer Key

The Answer Key for *Blueprints 2* is available on the Thomson Heinle website: elt.thomson.com/blueprints

ACKNOWLEDGMENTS

This book and its companion text *Blueprints 1* are the result of L2 writing, research, and discussion as well as L2 teaching experience and learning experience with writing. We would like to thank those educators and learners who helped us arrive at our current understanding of L2 writing by sharing their insights, teaching ideas, and learning hints.

The four of us offer a very special word of thanks to our editors who have been so great throughout the development of the *Blueprints* books. Huge thanks go to Susan Maguire, who has been a constant source of guidance and inspiration from the very inception of this series. Likewise, we are tremendously indebted to Kathy Sands Boehmer, who provided just the right amounts of positive feedback and gentle nudging throughout the completion of this project. In addition, we are forever grateful to our developmental editor, Kathleen Smith, whose careful editing and diligent work have played an integral role in the creation of this final product.

We would also like to thank the following reviewers who offered ideas and suggestions that shaped our revisions: Prof. Jim Bame, Utah State University; Carolyn Baughan, Illinois State University; Jane Curtis, Roosevelt University; Judy W. Davis, Oklahoma State University; Zeljana Grubisic, University of Maryland at Baltimore County; Jody Hacker, Missions College; Daryl Kinney, Los Angeles City College; Manuel Munoz; Michael Roehm, American University; Anne-Marie Schlender, Austin Community College.

Keith S. Folse
M. Kathleen Mahnke
Elena Vestri Solomon
Lorraine Williams

UNIT

1

Blueprints for

PARAGRAPH TO ESSAY

Blueprints for the Paragraph and the Essay

Objectives

In Part A, you will:

Analysis:

review the three basic parts of a paragraph

identify and analyze the three basic parts of an essay

learn about and analyze thesis statements

learn techniques for writing effective essay introductions, bodies, and conclusions

Unity and Coherence:

learn about unity and coherence in paragraphs and essays

Practice:

practice working with essay introductions, bodies, and conclusions

practice unity and coherence in writing

The Paragraph

One of the basic building blocks of academic writing is the **paragraph.** A paragraph is a group of sentences that work together to develop one main idea. The main idea is often stated in the first sentence of the paragraph, **the topic sentence.** The topic sentence includes the topic and a **controlling idea,** which gives a focus to the topic and often gives the reader information about the organization of the paragraph. After the topic sentence comes the **body.** Sentences in the body of the paragraph support or develop the main idea in the topic sentence. Most paragraphs end with a **concluding sentence.** This sentence either summarizes the ideas in the paragraph or acts as a transition to the next paragraph.

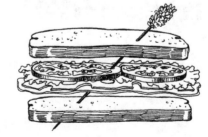

PARAGRAPH

Topic sentence

Body
(supporting sentences)

Concluding sentence

THE THREE PARTS OF THE PARAGRAPH

Read the paragraph and answer the questions.

WRITING FOR A PURPOSE

Paragraphs and essays are often categorized according to their purposes. One purpose is to explain a process. Writers use a process paragraph or essay to tell how to do something, for example, how to change a tire. Another purpose is to classify, and writers use classification paragraphs and essays to categorize things, for example, different kinds of insects or cars. A third purpose is to compare and contrast. Writers compare and contrast when they write about such things as choosing among jobs, movies, or investment strategies. Yet another purpose is to show cause and effect. Cause/effect paragraphs and essays analyze why things happen the way they do. A final and important purpose for writing is to give an opinion or argue a point of view. This purpose is the basis for much academic writing. Categorizing paragraphs and essays according to their purposes is a convenient and useful way of describing them.

1. Write the paragraph's topic sentence here. Circle the topic and underline the controlling idea.

   _____

   _____

2. Write one sentence here from the body of the paragraph.

   _____

   _____

   Does it support or develop the main idea in the topic sentence?

   _____

3. Write the paragraph's concluding sentence here.

   _____

   _____

   Does the concluding sentence summarize or relate to the topic sentence?

   _____

4. What is the primary purpose of this paragraph? (Circle one.)
   a. To explain a process
   b. To classify
   c. To state an opinion
   d. To discuss cause and effect

5. How many kinds of paragraphs are discussed in this paragraph?

_5_

List them here.

_____

_____

_____

_____

Unity and Coherence in Paragraphs

Unity and coherence are essential components of a good paragraph. They help your writing make sense and flow smoothly.

Unity

One characteristic of good writing is **unity.** Each paragraph you write, whether it stands alone or is part of a longer essay, should have unity. When a paragraph has unity, all of the sentences in it relate to the topic and develop the controlling idea. If a topic sentence states that a paragraph will be about how to prepare for a successful job interview, all sentences in the paragraph should talk about job interview preparation. Adding sentences about how to talk to your new boss once you are hired would destroy the paragraph's unity. Unity is important in all types of writing. In each unit in Blueprints 2, you will study techniques for planning and writing paragraphs and essays with unity.

EXERCISE

2

PARAGRAPH UNITY

Read each topic sentence. Draw a line through the sentence that does not support this topic sentence. On the blank line, explain your choice. The first one is done for you.

1. Topic sentence: The crow is a large black bird with some surprising characteristics.
   a. Many crows actually seem to enjoy being with people.
   b. Crows like to spend time communicating with one another and sometimes seem to have long and involved conversations.
   c. ~~The raven is a relative of the crow, but the two are very different.~~
   d. Crows also seem to feel sympathy when they see other injured birds.

   Explanation: _I chose C because it talks about ravens, but the topic of the paragraph is not ravens. It's crows._

2. Topic sentence: Life in the interior of Alaska is quite challenging in the winter.
   a. In the summer, the temperature outdoors averages a perfect 70 degrees Fahrenheit.
   b. For most of the winter, interior roads are closed to all vehicles except snowmobiles.
   c. Temperatures regularly dip to 40 or 50 degrees Fahrenheit below zero, making it impossible to go outside without special clothing.
   d. Fresh fruits and vegetables are unavailable in the winter, even for a premium price, so maintaining a balanced diet is a challenge.

   Explanation: _____

   _____

3. Topic sentence: To answer questions about the past, historians use different kinds of evidence.
   a. They examine primary sources, or firsthand written accounts of people who lived in the past.
   b. They use unwritten evidence—carvings, statues, ancient ruins, and the like—to piece together historical information.
   c. In the face of evidence, historians must determine what is accurate and what is false or biased.
   d. Historians also gather information from secondary sources, or accounts that have already been written about the historical events.

   Explanation: _____

   _____

Coherence

Another important characteristic of good writing is **coherence.** Coherent writing flows smoothly and ideas are arranged logically. There are many different ways to make your writing coherent.

Strategies for Coherence

1. Make sure you arrange your ideas in a logical order. Sometimes this will be chronological order. (See Unit 3, pp. 57–83.)

   Example:

   Incorrect: There are several steps involved in baking an angel food cake. After you sift the flour, add the sugar to it. First, sift the flour.

   Correct: There are several steps involved in baking an angel food cake. First, sift the flour. Then add the sugar to it.

2. Repeat key words, use appropriate pronouns, and use synonyms. (See Unit 6, pp. 147–149.)

Example:

I saw a very interesting **man** at **the supermarket** yesterday. **The supermarket** (repetition of key word) was a busy place, and everyone seemed to be in a hurry, except for **this customer** (synonym). There **he** (appropriate pronoun) stood, with a line of people behind him, blocking the produce aisle, gazing at the eggplants.

Transition Expressions

Use transition expressions to link your ideas together smoothly. Units 2, 3, 4, 5, and 7 each feature different transition expressions appropriate to that unit's essay type. Here is a small sampling:

Unit 3: You should put the egg in the water **first. Next,** heat the water until it boils.

Unit 5: A practice that has been around for almost three thousand years will certainly not disappear any time soon. **In fact,** the number of plastic surgery operations performed is growing steadily. **However,** before turning to the knife to alter physical appearance, it is important to ask the simple question, "Why?"

Unit 7: **Although it may be true** that there appear to be dry riverbeds on the planet Mars, this does not prove that water or life once existed there.

EXERCISE

3

ARRANGING IDEAS IN LOGICAL ORDER

In the following paragraph, the topic sentence and the concluding sentence are in the correct place. However, one or more of the supporting sentences is out of order. Make the paragraph coherent by rearranging the supporting sentences in the correct order.

COAL FORMATION

Topic Sentence: The coal we burn as fuel today began long ago as trees and other plants that grew beside water. (1) Movement of the rocks underneath then crushed some of the brown lignite coal even more and heated it, forming a hard black coal called *anthracite.* (2) Instead, they piled up, gradually forming a soft brown substance called *peat,* which was eventually buried. (3) When these plants died and fell to earth, they could not rot completely because the ground was too wet. (4) The peat was then crushed by its own weight and the weight of the rocks above it,

(continued)

(continued)

making it harder and turning it into *lignite,* or *brown coal.* **Concluding sentence:** This process of coal formation from living plants took place very slowly over millions of years.

Adapted from N. Curtis, M. Allaby, *Planet Earth*
(New York: Kingfisher Books, 1993) p. 74.

EXERCISE

4

REPEATING KEY WORDS AND SYNONYMS; USING APPROPRIATE PRONOUNS

Read the paragraph. Underline the key words and synonyms in the topic sentence and throughout the paragraph. Correct any incorrect use of pronouns.

AN AMAZING ANIMAL

On the way back to our hotel one night during our vacation on the beautiful island of Tasmania, my husband and I encountered a very strange animal. This animal had four legs and a furry body. At first they thought it was a beaver, because we also had a long flat tail. Then, however, we noticed something odd about its head. Instead of a beaver's mouth, you had a bill, like that of a duck or some other bird. What a strange thing! When we got back to our room, we asked the desk clerk for information about this peculiar beast because we both thought you were seeing things! We were relieved to find out that a furry mammal with a duck-like bill is not just a figment of their imagination. Strange as it may seem, such an animal actually does exist. Do you know what she is?

EXERCISE

5

USING TRANSITION WORDS

Circle the word or phrase that joins each pair of ideas coherently.

1. Angela loves chocolate; (however/for example), she really doesn't like ice cream.

2. (During/while) the movie, our power went out.

3. (Although/Not only) the West Nile virus has shown up in New York City, doctors are not too worried that it might move to other parts of New York.

4. In the last decade, much progress was made in the area of AIDS research; (nevertheless/in addition), there is still no cure for this deadly disease.

5. Hawaii has a moderate climate; (consequently/as), it never gets excessively hot or cold there.

NOTE: **You can stop here and practice paragraph writing before continuing on to the essay. See Appendix 1, p. 217, for paragraph writing topics and a checklist to guide you.**

The Essay

Most academic writing is longer than one paragraph. In fact, paragraphs are usually building blocks for **essays.** An **essay** is a group of paragraphs about one topic. Like a good paragraph, a good essay is unified and coherent. You can use the same techniques in both to achieve unity and coherence. You can classify essays and paragraphs according to the same purposes (process, cause/effect, etc.), but an essay contains more details and examples than a paragraph. Therefore, it is a larger piece of writing.

Each essay has three major parts: **an introduction, a body,** and **a conclusion.** These parts correspond to the three major parts of the paragraph, but they are longer. An essay's introductory paragraph contains some general statements about the essay topic as well as its **thesis statement.** The thesis statement, like a paragraph's topic sentence, gives focus to the essay, presents the controlling ideas of the essay, and provides information about the organization of the essay.

IMPORTANT NOTE:

Essays can be as short as three paragraphs or as long as 20 or 30 paragraphs. A common length for essays in college writing is four to seven paragraphs.

Each paragraph in the body of an essay supports the thesis statement. Each contains a topic sentence and supporting sentences that are linked together coherently and that develop the essay topic. The essay's conclusion, like the paragraph's concluding sentence, summarizes the essay's main ideas and brings it to an end.

EXERCISE

6

FROM PARAGRAPH TO ESSAY

A. *Read the paragraph and answer the question.*

JOB SKILLS

One way in which career counselors classify jobs is according to the broadly-defined categories of the skills that the jobs require. Counselors like to try to match these categories with areas of strength for those who seek the job. Counselors today consider three major skill categories: interpersonal skills, mental skills, and physical skills. Interpersonal skills help us establish and maintain personal relationships. We put them to use when we communicate with others, either in person or by other means. Mental skills are the skills of the mind. We use these skills when we process information, come up with and think through ideas, and plan how to transform ideas into actions. We rely on our physical skills when we use our hands or bodies. These are the skills that we need when we engage in the variety of physical activities that occur in our working lives. According to today's career counselors, it is important to think about our strengths in all three of these skill areas when we are trying to find a career that fits our needs.

The three categories of skills in this paragraph support the controlling idea, but they provide limited information. What kinds of details could the writer add to expand each category and make it more clear for the reader? Jot down some of your ideas here.

interpersonal skills: _____

_____

mental skills: _____

_____

physical skills: _____

_____

B. *Read the essay, which is an expanded version of the paragraph in part A. Then answer the questions.*

JOB SKILLS

sifting through:
examining carefully

Are you looking for a job? How do you go about **sifting through** the seemingly endless stream of information available to find that one job for you? Well, career counselors, who are trained to help people find their ideal jobs, can be very helpful in your job search. One way in which career counselors try to match people with their ideal jobs is according to the broadly-defined categories of skills that the jobs require. Counselors today consider three major skill categories: interpersonal skills, mental skills, and physical skills.

Interpersonal skills help us establish and maintain personal relationships. We put them to use when we communicate with others, either in person or by other means. For example, people who work in retail sales, real estate, or other merchandising areas need highly developed interpersonal skills. Interpersonal skills are also very important for people in the so-called "helping" professions—doctors, nurses, teachers, and social workers. In fact, today's medical schools are giving almost as much weight to the interpersonal skills of their applicants as they do to their mental skills when evaluating these candidates for acceptance into their training programs.

Mental skills are the skills of the mind. We use these skills when we process information, come up with and think through ideas, and plan how to transform ideas into actions. Mental skills are obviously important for writers, academics, and researchers. But these are not the only careers that demand high-level mental skills. Any job that involves helping people solve problems—from what color hat to choose to how to cope with

(continued)

insomnia: inability to sleep

stamina: endurance

dexterity: skill in physical movement, especially of the hands

(continued)

stress, depression, or **insomnia**—demands mental skills. These skills include such general abilities as synthesizing, analyzing, perceiving, and visualizing and are thus important in many fields.

We rely on our physical skills when we use our bodies. These are the skills that we need when we engage in the variety of physical activities that occur in our working lives. Physical skills involve such things as **stamina, dexterity,** and physical strength. These skills are especially important for people who spend their time moving, carrying, and lifting things. Athletes, mail carriers, truck drivers, farmers, ranchers, and others who work outdoors often must rely heavily on their physical skills.

Few jobs involve only one of the three major skill types; most jobs need all of them, at least to a certain extent. Even a computer programmer, who may sit for hours at a time in front of her computer, needs a key physical skill. Without finger dexterity, her job would be quite challenging! However, most jobs do require greater competence in one of the three skill areas than they do in the others. According to today's career counselors, it is important to think about our strengths in all three of these skill areas when we are trying to find a career that fits our needs.

1. Find the thesis statement of this essay and write it here.

   _____

   _____

   _____

2. Underline the topic sentence in each supporting paragraph.

3. How are the skill categories introduced in part A expanded upon and supported in the essay?
   a. by telling a story
   b. by giving examples and explaining them
   c. by introducing more major categories
   d. by describing the steps in a process

4. Does the author use any of the ideas you suggested in part A to expand this paragraph into an essay? If so, which ones?

   _____

   _____

   _____

EXERCISE 7

FROM PARAGRAPH TO ESSAY

Look again at the paragraph and the essay in Exercise 6. Write the sentences from the paragraph on the appropriate lines in the essay diagram below to illustrate the ways in which a paragraph can be expanded into an essay. Draw lines from the paragraph sentences to the diagram.

PARAGRAPH

JOB SKILLS

One way in which career counselors classify jobs is according to the broadly-defined categories of the skills that the jobs require. Counselors like to try to match these categories with areas of strength for those who seek the job. Counselors today consider three major skill categories: interpersonal skills, mental skills, and physical skills. Interpersonal skills help us establish and maintain personal relationships. We put them to use when we communicate with others, either in person or by other means. Mental skills are the skills of the mind. We use these skills when we process information, come up with and think through ideas, and plan how to transform ideas into actions. We rely on our physical skills when we use our hands or bodies. These are the skills that we need when we engage in the variety of physical activities that occur in our working lives. According to today's career counselors, it is important to think about our strengths in all three of these skill areas when we are trying to find a career that fits our needs.

ESSAY

INTRODUCTION

Thesis Statement: _____

_____

_____

BODY PARAGRAPH 1

Topic Sentence: _____

_____

_____

BODY PARAGRAPH 2

Topic Sentence: _____

_____

_____

BODY PARAGRAPH 3

Topic Sentence: _____

_____

_____

CONCLUSION

Concluding Sentence: _____

_____

_____

The Thesis Statement

The **thesis statement** of an essay is similar in purpose to the topic sentence of a paragraph. It presents the topic and the controlling idea for the entire essay. The thesis statement also often acts as a guide to other important information:

▶ the purpose and corresponding organizational structure of the essay

▶ the writer's point of view or opinion about the topic

IMPORTANT NOTE:

The thesis statement is the "key" to the essay. Without this key it is difficult to unlock the meaning of the essay.

Some thesis statements mention the subdivisions or subtopics that will be treated in the essay. Each of these subtopics then becomes a separate paragraph in the body of the essay. Other thesis statements do not provide the subtopics, but they indirectly say what they will be.

Direct Thesis Statement: The financial problems that small residential liberal arts colleges face are the direct result of a decrease in the number of college-age students nationwide, an increase in the proportion of those students who prefer technical and professional training over the traditional liberal arts, and the rapid and far-reaching effects of the distance education movement.

Indirect Thesis Statement: There are a number of causes for the financial problems that small residential liberal arts colleges face.

EXERCISE

THESIS STATEMENTS

Read the thesis statements and answer the questions.

1. Four major components make up the marketing mix of any successful business: the product itself, the product price, the means of product distribution, and the means of product promotion.

    a. What is the topic of this essay? _____

    _____

    b. What subtopics will be discussed? _____

    _____

    c. Is this a direct or an indirect thesis statement? _____

    _____

    d. How many paragraphs will there probably be in the body of this

    essay? _____

    _____

e. Does the writer express an opinion in this thesis statement?

_____

If so, what is it? _____

_____

2. Depression strikes an increasing number of people each year, and its effects can be devastating.

a. What is the topic of this essay?_____

_____

b. Is this a direct or an indirect thesis statement? _____

_____

c. What is the purpose of this essay? _____

_____

3. You only have to scratch the surface to see how damaging competitive sports really are to the overall psychological development of children.

a. What is the topic of this essay? _____

_____

b. Is this a direct or an indirect thesis statement? _____

_____

c. Does the author express an opinion in this thesis statement?

_____

If so, what is it? _____

_____

Essay Introductions

The **introduction** is what readers read first, so it is very important. The introduction presents the essay topic in general. In addition, through the thesis statement, the introduction guides the reader to the essay's overall organization and purpose. The introduction should also include a "hook," something that grabs readers' attention and makes them want to read further.

Techniques for Writing Essay Introductions

You can use many techniques for writing introductions. The ones described here are hooks to engage readers. You will practice them in later units.

1. **Posing an interesting or controversial question or questions.** (practiced in Unit 2) This technique works well as a hook to draw the reader into the essay. After writers pose the questions, they give general ideas and background information and, finally, the thesis statement.

Example:

What if you were to wake up tomorrow morning and have no memory of the past? How would you function? Would you even know who you were? As unlikely as this may seem, it is not impossible. More and more Americans are finding themselves suffering from memory loss, some of it quite fast and without warning. Although one contributor to memory loss is Alzheimer's disease, there are other major causes as well, which can be classified according to the symptoms they produce.

2. **Employing the funnel method.** (practiced in Unit 3) This is probably the most common technique to attract the reader. An introduction that uses the funnel method begins with general ideas about the topic. These ideas gradually become more and more focused until they reach their most specific and focused point in the thesis statement. The funnel method is very common in academic writing. It is not always the most attention-getting method, but it is very effective in introducing readers to complex topics.

Example:

Life in the twenty-first century is full of new challenges and opportunities. The pace of change in all areas of daily life makes it difficult to put these challenges and opportunities into perspective. Nevertheless, as the new millennium begins, it is important to take stock of where we have been, where we are today, and where we are going. One of the most obvious places to begin this process is by reviewing the evolution and impact of technology—the technology of the past, technology today, and, perhaps most important of all, the likely technology of our future.

3. **Using a relevant quotation.** (practiced in Unit 4) Writers who use this technique are careful to choose quotations written by authorities or by someone who says something especially relevant to their topic. They can then follow this quotation with related background information, which leads into the thesis statement.

Example:

"Life is just a bowl of cherries." This well-known, **anonymous** quotation is the **motto** of the optimist, the well-adjusted. It implies that life is full of "tasty" good things, ripe for the choosing, if only you **avail** yourself of the opportunity to pick from among them. However, what if you can't? What if life's cherries are there for the picking, but they always seem out of your reach. What if, for reasons you cannot comprehend, you cannot bring yourself to take advantage of the good things in life, only seeing life as a series of ever-worsening bad happenings. Such is the world of the clinically depressed. Depression strikes an increasing number of people each year, and its effects can be **devastating.**

4. **Making a startling or dramatic observation or describing a scene in a dramatic, humorous, or otherwise interesting way.** (practiced in Unit 5) Further background information then follows the "dramatic" hook of this opening, which then leads to the thesis statement.

Example:

He pounds down the court, ball in hands. **Deftly** sidestepping every obstacle in his path, he **barrels** toward the net. Nothing can stop him now. He leaps. For a split second, time stops, and this incredible athlete appears to be suspended in mid-air, his feet at least five feet above the floor. Then, suddenly, time starts again and the crowd begins to roar. Michael Jordan has done it again. He has made an extremely difficult **feat** seem effortless and natural, as though he were born with the ability to leap tall buildings in a single bound. The true story of this athlete's rise to stardom, however, is one of long suffering, hard work, and seemingly endless obstacles.

---

anonymous: unknown

motto: special saying

avail (oneself) of: make use of

devastating: very harmful

deftly: with great skill

barrel: move forward with strength

feat: achievement; accomplishment

5. **Turning an argument "on its head."** (practiced in Unit 7) This fairly sophisticated attention-getting introduction begins with a sentence or two presenting a point of view that is really the opposite of what the writer wants to say. At the end of this introduction, the writer overturns this idea completely and presents the thesis statement, which is the opposite of what he or she started with. This type of introduction is especially useful when the purpose of the essay is to give an opinion or make an argument.

take part in: participate in

proponent: someone in favor of something

overall: general

Example:

American children are exposed to and **take part in** competitive sports starting at a very early age. By participating in such sports as football, tennis, and basketball, **proponents** claim, children learn the skills necessary to survive in today's fiercely competitive world. You only have to scratch the surface, however, to see how damaging competitive sports really are to the **overall** psychological development of children.

EXERCISE

THE INTRODUCTION AND THE THESIS STATEMENT

Read the introduction and answer the questions.

"You are what you eat." This saying is true, to a great degree, for all of us. Most of the food we take in acts as fuel and is gradually digested and converted to the muscle and other types of tissue in our bodies. However, recent research has confirmed that some foods do more than merely contribute to our physical health; some foods are important to our emotional health as well. These foods are referred to by doctors and psychologists as "mood foods" or "comfort foods," and their importance to our overall health cannot be overestimated. The process by which mood foods act on our bodies to relieve stress and to promote an overall feeling of well-being is a three-step process.

1. Which "hook" technique is used in this introduction?

   _____

2. What is the thesis statement? Write it here.

   _____

   _____

3. Is this a direct or an indirect thesis statement?

   _____

The Body of the Essay

The **body** of an essay contains enough paragraphs to explain, discuss, or prove the essay's thesis statement. In each body paragraph the writer should discuss one aspect of the essay's main topic. Each body paragraph has its own topic sentence, supporting sentences, and a transition or concluding sentence. To ensure unity and coherence, good writers arrange the body paragraphs in logical order and join them with appropriate transition expressions that make them read smoothly.

EXERCISE

10

TOPIC SENTENCES FOR BODY PARAGRAPHS

Read each thesis statement. Then write two possible topic sentences for body paragraphs based on the thesis statement.

1. Four major components make up the marketing mix of any successful business: the product itself, the product price, the means of product distribution, and the means of product promotion.

   Topic Sentence for Body Paragraph 1: _____

   _____

   Topic Sentence for Body Paragraph 2: _____

   _____

2. Depression strikes an increasing number of people each year, and its effects can be devastating.

   Topic Sentence for Body Paragraph 1: _____

   _____

   Topic Sentence for Body Paragraph 2: _____

   _____

3. You only have to scratch the surface to see how damaging competitive sports really are to the overall psychological development of children.

   Topic Sentence for Body Paragraph 1: _____

   _____

   Topic Sentence for Body Paragraph 2: _____

   _____

Essay Conclusions

The conclusion in an essay is the last paragraph or two. One purpose of all conclusions is to signal the end of the essay. Here are some other purposes for conclusions:

IMPORTANT NOTE:

One thing you should NOT do in a conclusion is introduce and begin discussing a new topic. If you do, you will leave the reader with an unfinished feeling and distract from the unity of the essay.

- ▶ to add coherence by summarizing or restating the essay subtopics
- ▶ to add coherence by restating the essay thesis
- ▶ to leave the reader with the writer's final opinion
- ▶ to make a prediction or suggestion about the topic of the essay

Conclusions: Purposes

Read the introduction and the conclusions. Then answer the questions.

Introduction: American children are exposed to and take part in competitive sports starting at a very early age. By participating in such sports as football, tennis, and basketball, proponents claim, children learn the skills necessary to survive in today's fiercely competitive world. You only have to scratch the surface, however, to see how damaging competitive sports really are to the overall psychological development of children.

Conclusion I: As has been demonstrated above, competitive sports can cause severe psychological damage to children. Research shows that, in a society that overvalues the "competitive edge," children can easily lose self-confidence and self-motivation when they are forced to engage in competitive sports at which they cannot succeed. In addition, children who are particularly successful in the competitive arena can develop aggressive tendencies which can manifest themselves in adult life as hostility and lack of empathy.

1. What purposes does this conclusion have? (Circle all that apply.)
    a To add coherence by restating the essay's thesis statement.
    b. To add coherence by restating important essay subtopics.
    c. To leave the reader with the writer's opinion.

Conclusion II: As has been demonstrated above, competitive sports can cause severe psychological damage to children. In a society which overvalues the "competitive edge," children can easily lose self-confidence and self-motivation when they are forced to engage in competitive sports at which they cannot succeed. In addition, children who are particularly successful in the competitive arena can develop aggressive tendencies which can manifest themselves in adult life as hostility and lack of empathy. In my view, this concentration on competition has become an epidemic in American culture. If something is not done in the near future to curb the American appetite for competitive sports, the youth of today will be unable to function as caring, productive members of the adult world of tomorrow.

2. What new purpose(s) have now been added to this conclusion? (Circle all that apply.)
    a. To restate the essay's thesis statement.
    b. To make a prediction about the essay's topic.
    c. To leave the reader with the writer's opinion.

3. Which of these two conclusions do you find the most interesting and effective? Why?

    _____

    _____

    _____

    _____

UNITY IN CONCLUSIONS

Read each thesis statement, the topic sentences for the body paragraphs of the essay, and the conclusion. Some conclusions have unity. Others include sentences that introduce new topics and do not have unity. Cross out any sentences in the conclusion that do not belong. (If you want further practice with paragraph writing, develop the topic sentence for each body paragraph into a full paragraph.)

1. *Thesis Statement:* Many facts about the personal life of Albert Einstein surprise us when we first learn about them.

   Topic sentences for body paragraphs:

   a. His treatment of women is surprising.
   b. His social awkwardness is surprising.
   c. Some of his political views are surprising.

Conclusion: People are often quite surprised to hear these aspects of Einstein's personal life. When they learn of them, they sometimes ask themselves such questions as: How could such a great scientist have such disregard for the women in his life? What caused this super-intellect to be so awkward in the most basic of social situations? And, how could this man whose science led almost directly to the development of the atom bomb be so opposed to war? Einstein, who loved all things simple, would be pleased with the simplicity of the answers to these questions: for all his greatness, Albert Einstein was still a human being subject to all of the same strengths and weaknesses as the rest of humankind. Nobody is perfect. Many other scientists, including Robert Oppenheimer, also had imperfect personal lives.

2. *Thesis statement:* According to health and fitness experts, snowshoeing has recently become a favorite winter sport among college students for three reasons: it is inexpensive, it is not dangerous, and it is a quiet, calming activity.

   Topic sentences for body paragraphs:

   a. Snowshoeing costs very little, making it affordable even for students with no income.
   b. Compared to skiing and snowboarding, snowshoeing is quite safe.
   c. Finally, many students like snowshoeing because it is a quiet sport that allows them to appreciate the calm and peacefulness of winter outdoors.

Conclusion: For all of the reasons discussed above, snowshoeing is becoming more and more popular among college-age students as a winter sport. Health and fitness experts recommend it to anyone who is looking for an affordable, safe, and quiet way to work off energy and enjoy the great outdoors during the long winter months.

3. *Thesis statement:* There are five important, albeit time-consuming, steps to successfully painting a room.

Topic sentences for body paragraphs:

a. First, all exposed surfaces that you don't want to paint need to be protected.
b. Next, you need to prepare the surfaces that you do want to paint.
c. "Cutting in" with a small brush is the first step in the actual painting.
d. Once you have cut in, you can use a roller to paint the large surfaces.
e. Cleaning up is the final step, and it is also very important.

Conclusion: As you can see, it is important to work carefully and methodically when you are painting a room. If you patiently follow the five steps outlined, you will have a beautiful product to show for your labor, and you can sit back, relax, and enjoy your beautiful room for years to come. The initial investment of a little extra time makes it all worthwhile in the end.

The Writing Process: Practice Writing an Essay

Objectives

Prewriting:	
Planning:	
Partner Feedback:	
First Draft:	
Partner Feedback:	
Final Draft:	

In Part B, you will:

brainstorm ideas about a topic

use an outline to organize your introduction, body, and conclusion

review classmates' outlines and analyze feedback

write an introduction, a body, and a conclusion

review classmates' essays and analyze feedback

use feedback to write a final draft of your essay

The Writing Process: Writing Assignment

Your assignment is to write an original essay of four to five paragraphs describing a person you admire. The person can be someone you know well or someone you don't know at all. Follow the steps in the writing process in this section.

Mother Teresa

Paul McCartney

Grandmother

Mr. Kelley

Prewriting: Brainstorming

Brainstorming can help you get ideas for writing. You can brainstorm with a group or a partner—which can often generate more ideas faster—or you can brainstorm by yourself. To brainstorm, think of as many ideas as possible about a topic. Write the ideas as they come to you without evaluating, connecting, or editing them.

For this essay assignment, choose a person you admire. On a separate sheet of paper, quickly write whatever comes to mind about this person: What does he or she look like? Why do you admire this person? What do you know about this person? Don't worry about ranking or sequencing your ideas for now. Just try to think of as many ideas as you can.

Planning: Outlining

The next step is to organize and plan your essay. You will also generate more ideas in this step. One of the most effective ways to organize ideas is to prioritize them and make an outline.

Prioritizing and Connecting Ideas from Your Brainstorming

Read over your brainstorming ideas. Which ideas go together? Which ones are the most important? Divide your ideas into three or four major groups and use them to fill in the outline that follows. Eliminate ideas that don't seem important or useful.

EXERCISE

13

OUTLINING

Before you fill in this outline, try to think of a thesis statement and a hook for your essay. If you can't think of these right now, don't worry. You can come back to them later.

ESSAY OUTLINE

Topic: _____

I. Introductory Paragraph Using One of the Techniques in Part A (pp. 15–17)
    A. Hook and Background Information

    _____

    B. Thesis Statement

    _____

II. Body Paragraph 1
    A. Topic Sentence

    _____

    B. Supporting Details

    _____

III. Body Paragraph 2
    A. Topic Sentence

        _____

    B. Supporting Details

        _____

IV. Body Paragraph 3 (optional)
    A. Topic Sentence

        _____

    B. Supporting Details

        _____

V. Concluding Paragraph with Clear Purpose(s) and Link to Thesis

    A. _____

        _____

    B. _____

        _____

Partner Feedback Form 1

Exchange outlines with another student. Read your partner's outline and answer the questions on Partner Feedback Form 1: Unit 1, p. 219, in Appendix 3. Discuss your partner's reactions to your outline. Make notes about anything you need to change before you write your paper. For more information about giving partner feedback, see Appendix 2, p. 218, Guidelines for Partner Feedback.

First Draft

You are now ready to write the first draft of your essay. Review your outline and any comments from your partner before you begin.

EXERCISE

14

WRITING THE INTRODUCTION

Write an introduction for your topic, using your outline and the feedback you received from your partner. Use one of the introductory techniques explained on pp. 15–17. End your introduction with a well-constructed thesis statement. When you finish, use this checklist to review your work.

Introduction Checklist

	YES	NO
▶ Did I use a hook?	☐	☐
▶ Does my introduction flow logically from general to more specific?	☐	☐
▶ Does my thesis statement provide the reader with a clear guide for the rest of the essay?	☐	☐
▶ Is the purpose of my essay clear?	☐	☐

What is it? _____

EXERCISE

15

WRITING BODY PARAGRAPHS

Review your outline and your introduction. Then write the body paragraphs. Remember that each paragraph should be about something mentioned in the thesis statement. When you finish, use this checklist to review your work.

Body Paragraph Checklist

	YES	NO
▶ Does each paragraph in my essay treat only one main idea?	☐	☐
▶ Does each contain a topic sentence with a clear controlling idea?	☐	☐
▶ Does each paragraph end with a logical concluding sentence?	☐	☐
▶ Do my body paragraphs all relate to and support the essay's thesis statement?	☐	☐
▶ Are all the supporting sentences in my body paragraphs relevant to the topic? That is, do they have unity?	☐	☐
▶ Are my body paragraphs arranged in a logical order? That is, do they have coherence?	☐	☐

EXERCISE	
16	

WRITING A CONCLUSION

Review again your essay outline, introduction, and body. Then write a conclusion for your essay. When you finish, use this checklist to review your work.

Conclusion Checklist

	YES	NO
► Does my conclusion successfully signal the end of my essay?	❑	❑
► Does my conclusion add coherence to the essay by		
a. restating the essay thesis?	❑	❑
b. summarizing or restating the essay subtopics?	❑	❑
► Does my conclusion:		
a. leave the reader with my final opinion?	❑	❑
b make a prediction or suggestion about the essay's topic?	❑	❑

Partner Feedback Form 2

Exchange essays with another student. Read your partner's essay and answer the questions on Partner Feedback Form 2: Unit 1, p. 221, in Appendix 3. Discuss your partner's reactions to your essay. Make notes about anything you need to change before you write your second draft. For more information about giving partner feedback, see Appendix 2, p. 218, Guidelines for Partner Feedback.

Final Draft

Carefully revise your essay using all the feedback you have received: partner feedback review of your outline and essay, instructor comments, and any evaluation you have done yourself. Use the following checklist to do a final check of your essay. In addition, try reading your essay aloud. This can help you find awkward-sounding sentences and punctuation errors. When you have finished, add a title to your essay and neatly type your final draft. See Appendix 4, p. 246, for information about writing titles.

Final Draft Checklist

	YES	NO
▶ Does my introduction have an effective hook?	☐	☐
▶ Did I include a thesis statement that contains a clear topic and controlling idea?	☐	☐
▶ Does each of my body paragraphs have a clear topic sentence?	☐	☐
▶ Does each of my body paragraphs treat one subtopic?	☐	☐
▶ Did I use transition expressions between body paragraphs to help make the essay coherent?	☐	☐
▶ Does my concluding paragraph have clear purposes?	☐	☐
▶ Does my concluding paragraph successfully signal the end of my essay?	☐	☐
▶ Does my entire essay have unity and coherence?	☐	☐
▶ Does my essay have a title?	☐	☐

Additional Writing Assignments from the Academic Disciplines

Beginning with the Prewriting activity on p. 24, use the writing process to write another essay. Choose a topic from the following list.

SUBJECT	*WRITING TASK*
Business	Write about the company in your hometown that employs the most people. How did this company get so big? What is its history?
Science	Describe the duckbill platypus (or some other animal you are interested in). Write about its physical characteristics as well as its habitat and habits.
Technology	What is the impact of the Internet on third world countries? Give your opinion.
Literature	Choose a novel that you like. Explain the plot and why you like it so much.

UNIT
5

Blueprints for

CAUSE/EFFECT ESSAYS

Blueprints for Cause/Effect Essays

Objectives

In Part A, you will:

Analysis:

learn about methods of organization in cause/effect essays

Unity and Coherence:

Unity:

learn to focus on the relationship between causes and effects

Coherence:
Transition Expressions:

learn to use *because/as/since* + s + v; *therefore; consequently; thus; as a result* + s + v/*as a result of*

Grammar Focus:

do a verb tense review

Sentence Check:

study fragments, run-ons, and comma splices

Practice:

practice organizing causes and effects

What Is a Cause/Effect Essay?

In cause/effect essays, writers focus on what causes something (why it happens) and what the effects are (the consequences or results). For example, you might write an essay about what causes unemployment and its consequences, or about the causes of hurricanes and their consequences.

Methods of Organization

You can organize a cause/effect essay according to the information that you want to present. You can focus on 1) only the causes of something leading to one effect, 2) only the effects resulting from one cause, 3) more than one cause leading to more than one effect, or 4) a chain reaction of cause leading to effect leading to cause leading to effect. The charts below show the many options you can use when you organize a cause/effect essay.

Method 1: Causes leading to only one effect

Example thesis:

The main causes of unemployment in the United States are downturns in the economy, lack of vocational or professional skills, and personal choice to be unemployed.

Cause 1   Cause 2   Cause 3

Method 2: Effects resulting from only one cause

Example thesis:

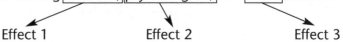

Unemployment can have terrible effects on individuals, including financial, psychological, and social difficulties.

Effect 1   Effect 2   Effect 3

Method 3: Many causes having many effects

Example thesis:

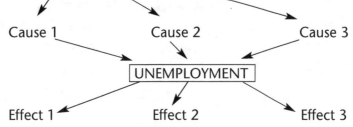

The numerous factors that lead to unemployment can have disastrous effects on individuals.

Cause 1   Cause 2   Cause 3

UNEMPLOYMENT

Effect 1   Effect 2   Effect 3

Method 4: A chain of causes leading to effect leading to cause leading to effect

Example thesis:

The loss of a job can sometimes lead to extreme actions such as suicide.

Cause ➤ Effect . . . Cause ➤ Effect... Cause ➤ Effect

In this example, you would trace the causes and effects that could lead from unemployment to suicide.

NOTE: Later in this unit, you will be asked to choose one of the four methods to organize your cause/effect essay.

EXERCISE

1

RECOGNIZING METHODS OF ORGANIZATION

Each item provides information about planning a cause/effect essay. Read the information and circle the correct method of organization. Refer to the methods of organization above for help.

1. *Thesis Statement:* Young people join the military for many reasons.

   Body paragraph 1: One major reason is to get away from home.

   Body paragraph 2: Depending on the political climate, many young people join in order to serve their country.

Body paragraph 3: Because of the excellent educational support that the military offers, some people join to get university scholarships.

Method 1   **Method 2**   **Method 3**   **Method 4**

2. *Thesis Statement:* By winning the lottery, Dr. Kovacs became an influential politician.

Body paragraph 1: Dr. Kovacs won the lottery and was featured on television.

Body paragraph 2: Interviewers asked her questions ranging from her personal life to her political beliefs.

Body paragraph 3: Television viewers saw the interviews and liked the message Dr. Kovacs was giving.

Body paragraph 4: Because they liked the message, many people contacted Dr. Kovacs and suggested she run for office.

Body paragraph 5: Dr. Kovacs took their suggestion, ran for office, and won a seat on her local city council.

Method 1   **Method 2**   **Method 3**   **Method 4**

3. *Thesis Statement:* Daily reading has excellent benefits.

Body Paragraph 1: People who read daily increase their vocabulary.

Body Paragraph 2: Daily reading also causes an increased reading speed.

Body Paragraph 3: Depending on the information that is read, people who read daily increase their general and specific knowledge.

Method 1   **Method 2**   **Method 3**   **Method 4**

4. *Thesis Statement:* By practicing yoga, people can improve their physical, mental, and emotional well-being.

Body Paragraph 1: Yoga can improve physical strength.

Body Paragraph 2: To improve mental awareness, yoga exercises are very effective.

Body Paragraph 3: People who practice yoga tend to experience emotional well-being.

Method 1   **Method 2**   **Method 3**   **Method 4**

Unity in Cause/Effect Essays

A cause/effect essay should focus on one topic and explain causes and effects that are relevant to that topic. In other words, the focus should be sharp. To achieve unity, your readers need to be able to see clearly the relationship between causes and effects that you are presenting. (See Unit 1, pages 4–5 and 21–22 for more about unity in essays.)

EXERCISE

2

FOCUSING CAUSES AND EFFECTS

Read each thesis statement and the three statements that follow, which are either causes or effects. One of these cause or effect statements does not relate to the thesis. Work with a partner and circle the letter of the sentence that does not lend unity to the information.

1. THESIS: Learning a foreign language can have many positive benefits.

    a. A person can communicate with a wide variety of people.

    b. Learning a foreign language can also enhance one's understanding of another culture.

    c. Some languages are much more difficult to learn than others.

2. THESIS: Three main factors are connected with the onset of high cholesterol.

    a. High cholesterol is a dangerous affliction that can cause heart attacks.

    b. Some healthy people get high cholesterol through heredity when parents pass it down to children.

    c. High cholesterol can be attributed to unhealthy eating habits.

    d. Lack of exercise can also lead to a rise in cholesterol levels.

3. THESIS: Because of the sudden hurricane, the villagers are now migrating west.

    a. The hurricane caused massive destruction to homes and other buildings.

    b. Because the buildings were uninhabitable, the townspeople slept outdoors.

    c. These outdoor living conditions were very poor.

    d. The villagers applied for local, state, and federal aid.

    e. Aid was refused, so the villagers moved to other regions of the country.

Coherence in Cause/Effect Essays

In cause/effect essays, transition expressions help create coherence. (To review general information about coherence in essays, see Unit 1, pages 5–8.)

Transition Expressions

Transition Expressions: *because/as/since + s + v; therefore; consequently; thus; as a result + s + v/as a result of*

because/as/since + subject + verb

Function: to give the cause of or reason for something

Use: *Because, as,* and *since* are subordinating conjunctions. Because these conjunctions introduce a dependent clause, they are followed by a subject and a verb. Note that these clauses CANNOT stand alone as independent sentences.

Examples: <u>Because Rita was tired</u>, she came home early from work. OR
Rita came home early from work <u>because she was tired</u>.

<u>As the weather was too unpredictable</u>, we were unable to make plans for the picnic. OR
We were unable to make plans for the picnic <u>as the weather was too unpredictable</u>.

<u>Since the tuition for Yale University was too high,</u> John decided to study at the City University of New York. OR
John decided to study at the City University of New York <u>since the tuition for Yale University was too high</u>.

Punctuation note: When the dependent clause beginning with *because, as,* or *since* comes at the beginning of the sentence, put a comma after it.

therefore/ consequently/ thus + subject + verb

Function: to show the result of something

Use: *Therefore, consequently,* and *thus* are conjunctive adverbs. They connect the previous information (cause) to the following information (effect.) Because these adverbs introduce sentences (independent clauses), they are followed by a subject and a verb.

Examples: Rita was tired. <u>Therefore, she came home early from work.</u>

The weather was unpredictable. <u>Consequently, we were unable to make plans for the picnic.</u>

The tuition for Yale University was too high; <u>thus, John decided to study at the City University of New York.</u>

(continued)

(continued)

Punctuation note: When these transition words begin a new sentence, put a comma after the word. If the transition word connects one sentence to another, put a semicolon before the word and a comma after it.

as a result + s + v/as a result of

Function: to signal the effect of something

Use: *As a result* and *as a result of* are commonly used at the beginning of a sentence to show the effects or results of a previous action. *As a result* introduces an independent clause and is followed by a subject and a verb. *As a result of* is followed by a noun.

Examples: Rita was extremely tired. <u>As a result,</u> she went home from work early.

<u>As a result of</u> her fatigue, Rita went home from work early.

Punctuation note: *As a result* is followed by a comma.

Blueprint Cause/Effect Essays

In this section, you will read and analyze two sample cause/effect essays. These essays can act as blueprints when you write your own cause/effect essay in Part B.

Blueprint Cause/Effect Essay 1: **Marketing Health and Fitness**

PREREADING DISCUSSION QUESTIONS

1. *Have you ever been on a diet? If so, did it work well for you? Why or why not?*

2. *Do you think there is a "perfect" body type? Why or why not? Which body type do you think most people would call "perfect?"*

EXERCISE

3

READING AND ANSWERING QUESTIONS

Read the cause/effect essay. Then answer the questions that follow.

boom: increase; burst of growth

infiltrate: permeate; filter into

bombard: attack; continuously show

barrage: blast

emulate: imitate; copy

MARKETING HEALTH AND FITNESS

1   Americans spend between $30 and $60 billion a year on dieting. This amount is more than the gross national product for Morocco! Such spending has not always been the case. Only recently has the marketing **boom** on health, fitness, and dieting **infiltrated** American televisions, radios, and magazines. The message is clear: getting healthy through diet and exercise is a necessary part of life. As Americans continue to be **bombarded** with these health-conscious images, it is evident that the images have altered Americans' ideas about health. The current advertising trends in weight loss and fitness have had both positive and negative effects.

2   Perhaps the most positive effect of dieting and weight loss advertising is an increase in education. For many years Americans ate heavy foods cooked only in butter or lard. In addition, exercise was considered appropriate only for men. These trends changed as television and radio began promoting a healthier lifestyle that includes private gyms, low calorie foods, and aerobics tapes, among other things. As a result of this advertisement, Americans began to understand that diet, exercise, and other preventive measures made them healthier. They are now aware that heart disease and other illnesses can be controlled with proper diet and exercise. Since the media's attention to this phenomenon, Americans are certainly healthier than they were in the recent past.

3   Although the current trends in weight loss have made Americans more conscious of their health, they have also led to increased public pressure. This is true for teenagers, especially girls. Adolescents cannot escape the constant **barrage** of ads on television and radio and in magazines and newspapers. While some teenagers take this new-found knowledge and begin eating more appropriate foods and exercising regularly, others become obsessed with weight loss. As a result, these young people can develop eating disorders such as *bulimia* and *anorexia nervosa* to try to **emulate** the physiques of models and health promoters. In these cases, the focus on fit and healthy bodies has a negative effect.

4   The financial effects of health industry ads cannot be avoided. Americans spend billions of dollars each year trying to get fit. Consumers will spend whatever they have to in order to get the latest gym equipment, fat-free food, or diet supplement pill. Because all these marketing strategies promote healthy living, many people are spending excessive amounts of money on such products. Consequently, the diet industry continues to promote newer and 'better' products.

5   Marketing strategies have changed public opinion in many areas, and the idea that everyone should have a perfect body is a major example

(continued)

(continued)

of this. Knowledge is power, and Americans should learn as much as they can about health and fitness. Then they should use that knowledge in healthful ways.

POSTREADING QUESTIONS

1. *Read the hook (first sentence) of the essay. This is called a **dramatic statement,** an interesting piece of information that engages the reader to continue with the essay. In your opinion, why is this sentence dramatic?* This amount is more than the gross national product for Morocco!

2. *Read the thesis statement. Is it direct or indirect?* Indirect

3. *Refer to the methods of organization on pages 118–119. Which method does this essay use, 1, 2, 3, or 4?* 2

4. *How many effects are discussed in this essay?* 3

5. *Separate the effects into positive and negative.*
   Positive effect(s): Education

   Negative effect(s): financial

6. *In the conclusion paragraph, what is the author's opinion about the marketing of health products?* positive

Blueprint Cause/Effect Essay 2: Why Plastic Surgery?

PREREADING DISCUSSION QUESTIONS

1. *Do you know someone who has had plastic surgery? What kind of surgery did they have? Was it successful? Explain.*

2. *Would you ever consider having it done? Why or why not?*

EXERCISE
4

READING AND ANSWERING QUESTIONS

Read the cause/effect essay. Fill in the blanks with transition expressions from the list below. Use one of the words twice. Then answer the post-reading questions.

consequently   As a result of these operations   because   therefore

WHY PLASTIC SURGERY?

1   It seems impossible to imagine that the first cosmetic surgery was performed in antiquity, but it is true. By 3400 BC, Egyptians had already performed operations to reshape body tissues. Granted, the procedure of plastic surgery has undergone many changes and advancements since then, but one thing is clear. In today's society, people still want to alter their appearance for one reason or another. Just why are people **tempted** to undergo plastic surgery? The main reasons are for personal satisfaction, social acceptance, and professional advancement.

tempted: fascinated

2   The majority of people who **undergo aesthetic** plastic surgery say that they are doing it _____because_____ they want to feel better about themselves. These are people who, when they look in the mirror, see nothing but a huge nose or elephant ears. They don't necessarily care about what others think; _____therefore_____, they believe that they are going to feel better about themselves after having plastic surgery. These operations can range from small **nips and tucks** to complete makeovers. The bottom line is that the patients have an internal desire to please themselves.

undergo: experience

aesthetic: pleasing to the eye; beautiful

nips and tucks: minor plastic surgery procedures such as wrinkle reductions

(continued)

(continued)

conform: comply with; obey

3   Another cause for wanting plastic surgery is to **conform** to social norms. For example, some women dream of appearing "model-like." <u>Consequently</u>, they may have fat injected into their lips. Men are more likely to have their breasts reduced because they feel that their torsos are "unnatural" if their breasts are too meaty. These types of operations are often reflections of the current trends in body types.

4   Perhaps the most bizarre reason for plastic surgery is for professional development. While this phenomenon is not widely discussed, there are a number of people who alter their physical appearances in order to be more successful actors, dancers, or models. It is not uncommon to hear about starlets who have breast **augmentations** or, less frequently, breast reductions performed. <u>as a result of</u>, these people can be more "marketable."

augmentation: increase

5   A practice that has been around for almost three thousand years will certainly not disappear any time soon. In fact, the number of plastic surgery operations performed is growing steadily. However, before turning to the knife to alter physical appearance, it is important to ask the simple question, "Why?"

POSTREADING DISCUSSION QUESTIONS

1. What is the thesis statement of this essay? Write it here.

_____

2. The introductory paragraph contains a dramatic statement as a hook. In your opinion, why is the beginning of the essay dramatic?

_____

3. The controlling idea of a topic sentence is the idea that will be discussed in the paragraph. Write each of the controlling ideas discussed in the essay.

Paragraph 2: _____

Paragraph 3: _____

Paragraph 4: _____

4. *Read the conclusion. Is there any information from the conclusion that can be connected to the hook, or dramatic statements, of the essay? If yes, what is it?* _____

_____

Grammar Focus and Sentence Check

Grammar Focus: Verb Tense Review

The three main verb tenses are the present, the past, and the future. Within these tenses are several different options.

Present tense

1. The simple present is used for things that are generally known to be true.

   Examples: Water *boils* at 212 degrees Fahrenheit.

   The planets *rotate* around the sun.

   The simple present can also be used for events that are true now.

   Examples: Harold *works* at IBM.

   My mother and father *are* on vacation.

2. The present progressive (or present continuous) takes the form *(am/is/are)* + **MAIN VERB** + *ing*. It is used to describe what is happening at this moment.

   Examples: Brittany and Lisa *are watching* TV.

   The dogs *are barking* and *waking* up all the neighbors.

3. The present continuous can also describe an action that will occur in the immediate future. In this usage, the actual time is usually stated directly (see underlined parts of the sentence).

   Examples: I *am going* to the mall <u>this afternoon.</u>

   The members of the European Community *are meeting* in the Hague <u>in a few weeks.</u>

Present perfect tense

The present perfect takes the form *have/has* + past participle of the main verb. Because of its many uses, the present perfect can fall into three general categories: 1) indefinite past, 2) repeated past action, and 3) continuation of an action from the past to now.

Examples:

1. indefinite past tense

    Brianna *has seen* that movie. (She saw that movie at some unspecified time in the past.)

2. repeated past action, which may or may not happen again

    The Brazilian National Soccer Team *has won* the World Cup at least four times. (The action was repeated in the past.)

3. continuation of an action from the past to now

    The French language students *have studied* together since January. (They began to study in the past and continue in the present. This form is usually expressed with *since* and *for.* Common verbs for this usage are *live, study, work,* and *wear.*)

Past tense

1. The past tense describes actions that happened in the past. The simple past refers to an action that is finished. It began and ended in the past.

    Examples: John F. Kennedy *died* in 1963.

    I *finished* the book last night.

2. The past tense can also take the progressive form of *was/were + MAIN VERB + ing*

    This tense is commonly used for an action that was happening at a specific time in the past.

    Example: Last night at 7:30 I *was eating* dinner with my family.

    The past progressive can also explain an action that was interrupted by something (usually another action). The interruption often includes the word *when.*

    Example: We *were studying* in the library *when* the fire alarm went off.

    When you refer to two things that occurred at the same time, use *while* with the first action and put both verbs in the past progressive.

    Example: While the instructor *was grading* the essays, the students *were taking* a grammar test.

Future tense

Form the simple future most often by using the modal verb *will* + *MAIN VERB*.

> *Example:* The congressional leaders *will meet* in the near future to discuss the proposed bill.

Another way of forming the simple future tense is to use *be going to* + *MAIN VERB*.

> *Example:* The congressional leaders *are going to meet* in the near future to discuss the proposed bill.

EXERCISE

5

IDENTIFYING VERB TENSES IN ESSAYS

Reread Blueprints Essay 1 on pp. 124–125. Then answer the questions.

1. Find the sentences in paragraph 1 that use the present perfect tense. Underline them.

2. In paragraph 2, which two verb tenses are used?

_____

Reread Blueprints Essay 2 on pp. 126–127. Then answer the questions.

3. Find the sentence in paragraph 1 that uses the past perfect. Underline it.

4. In paragraph 2, find the sentence that uses the future tense. Write it

here. _____

EXERCISE

6

WORKING WITH VERB TENSES

Read the following sentences. In the blanks, write the correct form of the verb that is shown in parentheses ( ).

1. Belinda and her brother (work) *are working* in the library

   right now, but they (be) *will be* home later this evening.

2. The people who take the subway usually (commute)

   commute to the city but (live) *live* in the

   suburbs.

3. What time do your parents usually (wake up) *wake up* in

   the mornings?

4. Don't talk to Gretchen right now. She (watch) *is watching*

   her favorite program on TV.

5 How many times (Bob see) _has Bob seen_ that movie?

6. Yesterday while the students (talk) _were talking_ to the professor, she (look) _was looking_ in the textbook.

WORKING WITH VERB TENSES AND TRANSITION EXPRESSIONS

Read the following sentences. In the blanks, write the correct form of the verb that is shown in parentheses ( ). Then rewrite each sentence to include one of the transition expressions listed. The first one is done for you.

because   as a result of   therefore   since   consequently

1. We (want) _wanted_ to go to the beach yesterday, but it (be) _was_ too cloudy.

   Because it was too cloudy, we didn't go to the beach

   yesterday.

2. Dr. Goldstein's biology class (study) _was studying_ for the final exam for the past two weeks. The majority of the students did very well.

   therefore _____

   _____

3. My dog (chew) _____ my favorite shoes when I got home from work. I (be) _was_ so angry at her.

   Consequently _____

   _____

4. This afternoon Bill and Jim decided that the airline tickets to Pheonix (be) _were_ too expensive. They (decide) _decided_ to take a bus instead.

   _____

   _____

Sentence Check: Fragments, Run-ons, and Comma Splices

Three of the most common errors in English sentences are **fragments, run-ons,** and **comma splices.** It is important to learn to recognize and correct these errors.

Fragments

A fragment is an incomplete sentence. It is missing a crucial element, usually either the subject or the verb, and sometimes a whole clause. To correct a fragment, add the missing part.

Examples:

Fragment   Is a very nice day. (missing a subject)

Correction **It** is a very nice day.

Fragment   My birthday Tuesday. (missing a verb)

Correction My birthday **is** Tuesday.

Fragment   Because he wanted to lose weight. (missing an independent clause)

Correction **Mario joined a health club** because he wanted to lose weight.

Run-on Sentences

A run-on sentence contains two complete thoughts (two sentences) that are connected without any form of punctuation. To correct a run-on sentence, add punctuation between the two sentences or create two separate sentences.

Examples:

Run-on   Society has an obligation to help those in need this includes government support and privately funded donations.

Correction Society has an obligation to help those in need**;** this includes government support and privately funded donations.

Correction Society has an obligation to help those in need. **This** includes government support and privately funded donations.

Comma Splices

A comma splice is two sentences connected only by a comma. There are a few ways to correct a comma splice.

1. Put a semicolon (;) between the two sentences instead of a comma.

Example:

Comma splice   The effects of long-term exposure to the sun are not pleasant, people can suffer from skin cancer as well as from other epidermal illnesses.

Correction The effects of long-term exposure to the sun are not pleasant; people can suffer from skin cancer as well as from other epidermal illnesses.

2. Add a conjunction after the comma.

Example:

Correction The effects of long-term exposure to the sun are not pleasant, **for** people can suffer from skin cancer as well as other epidermal illnesses

3. Use a period to create two separate sentences.

Example:

Correction The effects of long-term exposure to the sun are not pleasant. **People** can suffer from skin cancer as well as other epidermal illnesses

EXERCISE

8

IDENTIFYING FRAGMENTS, RUN-ONS, AND COMMA SPLICES

Read the following sentences. Identify them as either fragments (FRAG), run-ons (RO), comma splices (CS), or correct (C)

__RO__ 1. In the freshman English class, the first semester focuses on writing the second semester focuses more on literature.

__FRAG__ 2. Because we were all extremely prepared for the final exam.

__C__ 3. The monastery's doors have been closed to the public for one hundred years.

__CS__ 4. Carol is not in law school; she's in medical school.

__FrAG__ 5. Since it was the first day of summer.

__C__ 6. The possibilities are endless, but the timing must be correct.

EXERCISE

9

CORRECTING FRAGMENTS, RUN-ONS, AND COMMA SPLICES

Reread the sentences in Exercise 8. Correct the fragments, run-ons, and comma splices. There may be more that one way to correct the errors.

EXERCISE

10

EDITING PRACTICE: GRAMMAR FOCUS AND SENTENCE CHECK APPLICATION

Read this paragraph carefully. Find and correct the eight errors in verb tense, fragments, run-ons, or comma splices. The first one is done for you.

Italians are becoming more and more angry at the sights they see on television, ~~in~~ almost every type of programming, models known as "soubrettes" or "letterine" were common sights. What do these women do? The answer, which upsets the majority of Italians, is . . . nothing. They stand on stage, wear extremely skimpy outfits, and pose for the camera. Appear on game shows, variety shows, sports shows, and even documentaries. While they are beautiful and, many argue, very nice to look at. They are having a negative effect on the youth of Italy. Adolescent girls are being encouraged to look good and nothing else. They didn't need entertainment skills such as singing, dancing, or interviewing, all that is required to become a soubrette is a hard body, full lips, and the ability to smile for the camera. With European unity in full swing, Italian mass media hopes to set the standard of quality television; however, with this type of programming, Italians will only succeed in becoming the laughing stocks of a united Europe.

@keilask

The Writing Process:
Practice Writing a Cause/Effect Essay

Objectives	In Part B, you will:
Prewriting:	practice using a spoke diagram to get ideas for your cause/effect essay
Planning:	use a chart to organize and sequence ideas
Partner Feedback:	review classmates' charts and analyze feedback
First Draft:	write a cause/effect essay
	use a dramatic statement as an introductory technique
Partner Feedback:	review classmates' essays and analyze feedback
Final Draft:	use feedback to write a final draft of your cause/effect essay

The Writing Process: Writing Assignment

IMPORTANT NOTE:

If an instructor in another class gives you an assignment that requires you to write a cause/effect essay, how do you know if you should write a cause-only essay, an effects-only essay, or an essay about both causes and effects? One way is to ask your instructor to put the assignment in question form, for example, "What were the reasons for the creation of the United Nations?" Even though the words *cause* and *effect* do not appear in the question, the topic is an effect (the creation of the United Nations) and you need to explain what the causes, or reasons, were.

Your assignment is to write an essay about the causes and effects of technological advances on a specific career or field of study. After you complete the Prewriting and Planning sections, you will decide whether your essay will follow method 1 (causes of technological advances), method 2 (effects of technological advances), or method 3 (causes and effects of technological advances). See pp. 118–119 to review these organizational methods. Then follow the steps in the writing process in this section.

Prewriting: Using a Spoke Diagram

A spoke diagram is a useful way of generating ideas for a cause/effect essay. In a spoke diagram, you put a topic in a central box or circle and draw arrows out from it, like the spokes on a wheel. Each arrow points to an idea that relates to the topic. The following questions may help you think of causes and effects that are related to your topic:

▶ How is this career or field of study different now from what it was 20 or 30 years ago?

▶ In what specific ways has this career or field of study changed?

▶ Why has it changed?

▶ What is different because of modern technology?

Here is a sample of a spoke diagram on the subject of illegal drugs in the Olympic Games. Notice that the writer includes ideas for both the causes of illegal drug use and the effects of it. The writer will not use all the ideas in the final essay.

**Topic: The causes and/or effects
of illegal drugs in the Olympic Games**

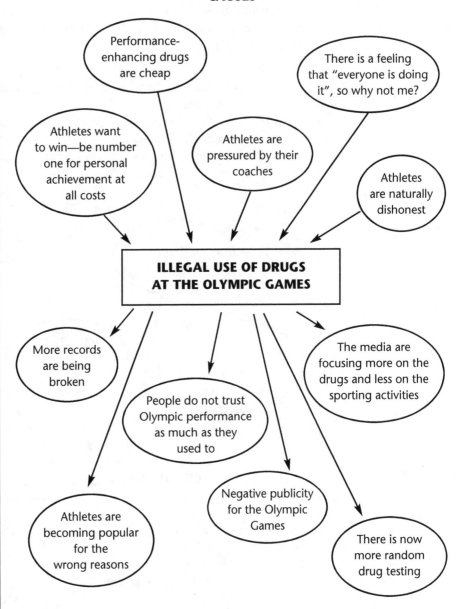

CAUSES

Performance-enhancing drugs are cheap

There is a feeling that "everyone is doing it", so why not me?

Athletes want to win—be number one for personal achievement at all costs

Athletes are pressured by their coaches

Athletes are naturally dishonest

ILLEGAL USE OF DRUGS AT THE OLYMPIC GAMES

More records are being broken

The media are focusing more on the drugs and less on the sporting activities

People do not trust Olympic performance as much as they used to

Athletes are becoming popular for the wrong reasons

Negative publicity for the Olympic Games

There is now more random drug testing

EFFECTS

CREATING A SPOKE DIAGRAM

Use the spoke diagram to record ideas for writing your cause/effect essay. The following steps will help you fill in the diagram. Remember that you will be eliminating some of these ideas in the planning stage, so just write everything you can think of now. If you need help with this diagram, look at the sample diagram on p. 137.

> STEP 1: Write the main subject of your essay (modern technology and a specific career or field of study) in the box in the center of the page.
>
> STEP 2: In the circles **above** your topic, write the CAUSES for the technology change.
>
> STEP 3: In the circles **below** your topic, write the EFFECTS of this technology change.

CAUSES

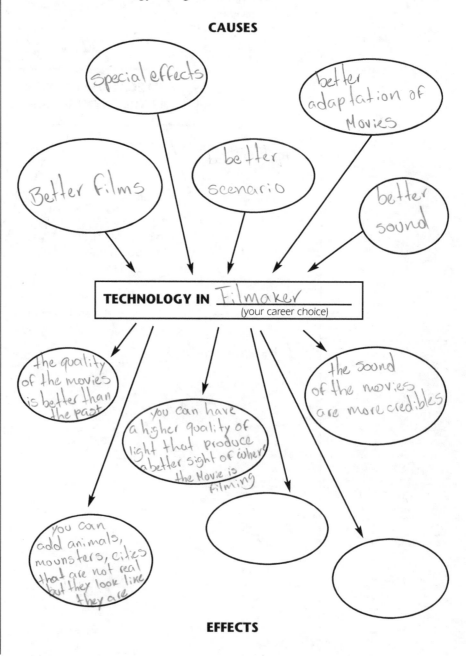

EFFECTS

Planning: Creating a Cause/Effect Chart

After the writer filled in her spoke diagram, she decided to plan the essay by organizing her information using a cause/effect chart. During this process, she discarded some of her original ideas and added some supporting details. Her chart ended up looking like this.

ILLEGAL DRUG USE IN THE OLYMPIC GAMES

CAUSES	EFFECTS
1. Athletes want to win.	1. More records are being broken.
Strong/unhealthy spirit of competition.	Give examples, names, dates
Want to be famous world-wide.	
2. Athletes are pressured by others.	2. There is more testing nowadays.
Ex: family, coaches, friends	Special organizations that test
Pressure from media	Random test results available
3. Athletes see others doing it.	3. People trust Olympic performance less.
Doesn't seem "bad"	Public disbelieving new records
Makes them equal to other athletes	Ex: Irish swimmer in 2000 games

In her chart, the writer was able to list supporting information for three causes and three effects of illegal drug use by athletes. As a result, she believes she has enough material to write an essay that will focus on both causes and effects. So she chooses Method 3 (causes and effects) as her essay's organizational method.

EXERCISE

12

FILLING IN A CAUSE/EFFECT CHART

Fill in the blank chart with causes and effects from your spoke diagram in Exercise 11. Then write as many supporting details as you can think of for each cause and each effect. When you are finished, follow the directions below the chart.

TECHNOLOGY AND _____

CAUSES	EFFECTS
1.	1.
2.	2.
3.	3.
4.	4.
5.	5.

Now review your chart. Did you list more causes than effects? Do your ideas seem stronger for effects than for causes? Are your lists evenly distributed? Depending on the answers to these questions, you can now choose which method of organization you will use: 1 (causes only), 2 (effects only), or 3 (causes and effects).

Cross out any ideas that you do not want to use. The remaining information in your chart will be the basis of your essay.

Partner Feedback Form 1

Exchange your cause/effect chart with another student. Read your partner's chart and answer the questions on Partner Feedback Form 1: Unit 5, p. 235, in Appendix 3. Discuss your partner's reactions to your chart. Make notes about any parts you need to change before you write your paper. For more information about giving partner feedback, see Appendix 2, p. 218, Guidelines for Partner Feedback.

First Draft

Now you are ready to write the first draft of your essay. Before you begin, review your cause/effect chart and any comments from your partner, especially the thesis statement suggestion.

EXERCISE

13

WRITING THE INTRODUCTION

Write an introduction for your topic, using your chart and the feedback you received from your partner. Use a dramatic statement as explained on p. 16, Unit 1 to begin your essay. Both "Marketing Health and Fitness" on pp. 124–125 and "Why Plastic Surgery?" on pp. 126–127 use this introduction technique. You can use them as models if you want. End your introduction with a well-constructed thesis statement. When you finish, use the checklist to review your work.

Introduction Checklist

IMPORTANT NOTE:

A dramatic statement can be any piece of interesting information about your topic. It can be a surprising statistic or statement, a brief story, or any other piece of interesting information that is related to your thesis statement.

• Try to make your dramatic statement surprising—something that your writer does not know about.

• Your dramatic statement should be followed by further background information that leads smoothly to the thesis statement.

	YES	NO
▶ Did I use an effective dramatic statement—a surprising fact or interesting story to introduce my topic?	☐	☐
▶ Does my introduction flow logically from the hook of the dramatic statement to the thesis?	☐	☐
▶ Does my thesis statement provide a clear indication of the Method of Organization I will use in the essay (1, 2, 3, or 4)?	☐	☐
▶ Is the purpose of my essay clear?	☐	☐

What is it? _____

EXERCISE

14

WRITING BODY PARAGRAPHS

Look again at your chart for your cause/effect essay. Then complete the body paragraphs. When you finish, use the checklist to review your work.

Body Paragraph Checklist

	YES	NO
▶ Does each body paragraph in my essay treat only one main idea?	☐	☐
▶ Does each contain a topic sentence with a clear controlling idea?	☐	☐
▶ Does each paragraph end with a logical concluding sentence?	☐	☐
▶ Do my body paragraphs all relate to and support the thesis statement of the essay? In other words, do they each discuss a cause and/or effect mentioned in my thesis statement?	☐	☐
▶ Are the relationships between causes and effects clear to the reader?	☐	☐
▶ Are all the supporting sentences in my body paragraphs relevant to the topic? That is, do they have unity?	☐	☐

EXERCISE

15

WRITING A CONCLUSION

*Review again your **cause/effect chart,** partner feedback form, introduction, and body. Write a conclusion for your essay. When you finish, use the checklist to review your work.*

Conclusion Checklist

	YES	NO
▶ Does my conclusion successfully signal the end of my essay?	☐	☐
▶ Does my conclusion add coherence to the essay by:		
a. restating the essay thesis?	☐	☐
b. summarizing or restating the essay subtopics?	☐	☐
▶ Does my conclusion:		
a. leave the reader with my final thoughts?	☐	☐
b. offer a suggestion, an opinion, or a prediction about the topic of the essay?	☐	☐

Partner Feedback Form 2

Exchange essays with another student. Read your partner's essay and answer the questions on Partner Feedback Form 2: Unit 5, p. 237, in Appendix 3. Discuss your partner's reactions to your essay. Make notes about any parts you need to change before your write your second draft. For more information about giving partner feedback, see Appendix 2, p. 218, Guidelines for Partner Feedback.

Final Draft

Carefully revise your essay using all the feedback you have received: partner feedback review of your chart and essay, instructor comments, and any evaluation you have done yourself. Use the checklist to do a final check of your essay. In addition, try reading your essay aloud. This can help you find awkward-sounding sentences and errors in punctuation. When you have finished, add a title to your essay and neatly type your final draft. See Appendix 4, p. 246, for information about writing titles.

Final Draft Checklist

	YES	NO
▸ Did I use a dramatic statement to introduce the essay?	❏	❏
▸ Will my dramatic statement hook my audience?	❏	❏

Why or why not? _____

▸ Did I include a thesis statement that contains a clear topic and controlling idea?	❏	❏
▸ Is my method of organization obvious?	❏	❏
▸ Did I use transition expressions correctly?	❏	❏
▸ Did I use verb tense correctly?	❏	❏
▸ Are my sentences free of run-ons, fragments, and comma splices?	❏	❏
▸ Does each of my body paragraphs have a clear topic sentence?	❏	❏
▸ Does each body paragraph contain one subtopic?	❏	❏
▸ Does my concluding paragraph successfully signal the end of my essay? That is, does my concluding paragraph sound like a "final" paragraph?	❏	❏
▸ Does my entire essay have unity and coherence?	❏	❏

Additional Writing Assignments from the Academic Disciplines

Beginning with the Prewriting activity on p. 136, use the writing process to write another cause/effect essay. Choose a topic from the following list.

SUBJECT	*WRITING TASK*
Business	What are the effects of penny stocks on investors?
Science	What are the causes of a particular disease?
Technology	What are the effects on both high school students and admissions offices of submitting college applications on the Internet?
Geology	What are the causes and/or effects of earthquakes?
Current Issues	What are the causes and/or effects of homelessness?

UNIT
6

Blueprints for

REACTION ESSAYS

Blueprints for Reaction Essays

Objectives

	In Part A, you will:
Analysis:	identify and analyze a reaction essay
Unity and Coherence:	
Unity:	learn about background to unify a reaction essay
Coherence:	practice repeating key terms or phrases, using a pronoun to refer to a previous noun or noun phrase, and using synonyms
Grammar Focus:	study word forms
Sentence Check:	study sentence variety
Practice:	organize and write a reaction essay

What Is a Reaction Essay?

A very common type of writing task, one that appears in every academic discipline, is the **reaction essay.** In a reaction essay, the writer is usually given a prompt—a visual or written stimulus—to think about and respond to. A reaction essay focuses on the writer's feelings, opinions, and personal observations about the particular prompt.

!

IMPORTANT NOTE:

A prompt can be any number of things: a unit from a textbook, a piece of literature, a theory, a song, a picture, an article, a television program, a lecture, etc. Your instructor will often provide you with a prompt to generate the reaction essay.

EXERCISE

1

PRACTICING REACTIONS

Practice writing short reactions to the following stimuli. As you look at the pictures or read the item, answer these questions: How do you feel? What emotions are you experiencing? Explain why. Then compare your answers with a classmate's.

1. _____

    _____

    _____

    _____

    _____

2. "To be or not to be; that is the question."—William Shakespeare

_____

_____

_____

_____

_____

3.

4.

ANNOUNCEMENT:

Starting next semester, all first-year students will be required to do community service as part of their college education. Please contact the office for more information.

Dean of Undergraduate Studies

Unity in Reaction Essays

In order to create unity in a reaction essay, it is important to give the reader some background information about the prompt before you react to it. This background aids the reader in understanding what you are reacting to. It is important to maintain objective thought in the background information. The body of the essay will focus on your personal reaction, but you should begin with background information. (See Unit 1, pp. 4–5 and 21–22, for more about unity in essays.)

Background information varies based on the type of stimulus you are reacting to.

1. *Description:* If you are reacting to a *visual prompt,* the background information is usually a physical description of the item.

2. *Summary:* If you are reacting to a *written prompt,* you can give a summary of it in the introduction. Present the most important elements and follow the order of the original.

3. *Facts:* If you are reacting to a historical *event* or a *theory,* give factual information about it: specific dates, times, actions, and circumstances.

IMPORTANT NOTE:

You may want to use a combination of description, summary, and facts as background information in your introductory paragraph.

EXERCISE

2

CATEGORIZING BACKGROUND INFORMATION

Read the following reaction essay prompts. Working with a partner, decide if the background information should be a summary, *a* description, *or* factual information. *More than one answer is possible. The first one is done for you.*

1. the book *A Farewell to Arms* _summary_

2. the painting *Mona Lisa* _description_

3. the Battle of the Bulge in World War II _factual_

4. the song *Give Peace a Chance* _Summary_

5. the movie *To Kill a Mockingbird* _Summary_

6. the lecture "Developing Countries and their Economic Needs"
   Summary

7. a rejection letter from a university _factual_

Coherence in Reaction Essays

In reaction essays, you create coherence with key terms, pronouns, and synonyms. (To review general information about coherence in essays, see Unit 1, pp. 4–8).

Coherence Techniques

1. Repeating Key Terms or Phrases. This helps readers stay focused on the subject you are discussing.

   Examples:

   The use of *symbolism* in Lisa's short story was fascinating. This *symbolism* was found throughout the story.

   The *Concorde* is the fastest passenger jet in the world. However, after a terrible crash in 2000, many people wondered if the *Concorde* was a safe airplane.

2. Using a pronoun to refer to a previous noun or noun phrase.

   This method adds coherence by helping readers clearly follow the flow of information.

   Examples:

   Rhonda shocked everyone in her family. She decided to become a hot-air balloonist.

   The *system* of checks and balances is used to guarantee that none of the three branches of government has too much power. It promotes equity of power.

3. Using synonyms. Synonyms help maintain coherence by avoiding unnecessary repetition of information.

   Examples:

   The *Olympic Games* are played every four years in different countries. This *international competition* involves thousands of athletes from around the world.

   J.D. Salinger became an international success for his *book The Catcher in the Rye*. This *novel* touched millions of young people's lives.

PRACTICING COHERENCE

*Read the following paragraphs. Underline and identify the three coherence devices and write KT (repetition of key term), P (pronoun), or S (synonym) above them. **The first two readings have the key words underlined to help you.***

1. Dr. Louis' lecture took place at 8 P.M. last night. His important lecture covered a wide variety of historical topics, including political warfare in Africa and its effects on the local population. This conflict has been going on for more than twenty years, and it will probably continue for the foreseeable future.

2. The TOEFL® is a trademarked exam created by Educational Testing Service. This exam evaluates student performance in the skills of listening comprehension, grammar and written expression, reading comprehension, and, more recently, essay writing. These skills are R necessary in order to achieve academic success in university settings. The TOEFL® is widely used in the United States and Canada, and it P is administered through testing centers around the world.

3. I wonder who the creator of the hourglass was. I wonder how this person changed people's lives by this invention. What did they use it for? Did they appreciate this hourglass or end up resenting it?

4. Although many people in Europe and Asia still smoke, this habit is becoming more and more taboo. Lawmakers are now prohibiting smoking in public areas. These countries are realizing the actual risk that cigarette smoke has to nonsmokers. A steep decline in public smoking areas will definitely improve people's health.

Blueprint Reaction Essays

In this section, you will read and analyze two sample reaction essays. These essays can act as blueprints when you write your own reaction essay in Part B.

Blueprint Reaction Essay 1: **The Hourglass and Me**

PREREADING DISCUSSION QUESTIONS

1. What is the object pictured? hourglass

2. What is its purpose? Mesure the time

3. What do you feel when you look at this picture? that the life is too short.

EXERCISE

4

READING AND ANSWERING QUESTIONS

Read the reaction essay. Then answer the questions that follow.

THE HOURGLASS AND ME

1 Its shape is rather simple. It is rounded at the top and the bottom but pinched in the middle. Inside it are **fine grains** of sand. This is not a **static** object. The grains fall slowly but **persistently** from the upper portion to the lower portion. The hourglass, used to measure time, has a lot more meaning to me besides being a timepiece.

2 When I look at an hourglass, one of the primary images that comes to mind is history. Before the days of accurate timepieces, people had to use *something* that measured time. I wonder who the creator of the hourglass was. I wonder how the lives of people were changed by this invention. What did they use it for? Did they appreciate this hourglass or end up **resenting** it?

3 On a more personal level, the hourglass gives me a feeling of futility. Time is passing, and I can see it. It is right there in front of me. I cannot lie to myself and tell myself that I will do what I need to do tomorrow or the next day. I had better hurry up and do something with my life before the grains of sand have all fallen through the **crevice**. The picture is there, and it does not lie. I cannot escape time.

4 The reaction I feel from looking at an hourglass is also appreciation of simple beauty. The **exotic** curves of the glass flow so smoothly that I feel this hourglass is a living thing, not man-made. There really is something beautiful about the hourglass shape. It calls to me, and I end up feeling close to this innocent-looking device. It is clean and pure.

5 While the hourglass is not a classic piece of art, this small simple mechanism carries with it much power. The thoughts and emotions that come to my mind as I see it stimulate my sense of self. The power of the hourglass is inspiring.

1. Reread the introductory paragraph. What background method is used to introduce the topic? _Description_____

2. Read the thesis statement. Is it general or specific?

   _General_____

   What will the essay discuss? _Meanings_____

   _____

---

fine: very small

grains: small particles

static: unmoving; stagnant

persistently: in the manner of not stopping

resenting: feeling insulted; taking offense; disliking

crevice: gap; small opening; fissure

exotic: strikingly unfamiliar or unusual

3. What three reactions does the writer present in the body paragraphs?

   Body paragraph 1 _____

   Body paragraph 2 _____

   Body paragraph 3 _____

4. Read the sentences below from the essay. Which coherence method (repetition of key terms, pronoun, synonym) is being used in each example?

   a. "While the hourglass is not a classic piece of art, this small, simple mechanism carries with it much power." ___P, S___

   b. "Time is passing, and I can see it. . . . I cannot escape time."

   _____

5. Reread body paragraph 4. The author uses many adjectives in discussing the hourglass. Write five (5) of these adjectives here.

   Simple beauty, The exotic curves,
   living thing, man-made
   something beautiful, clean and pure
   innocent-looking device

   _____

6. In the concluding paragraph, what does the author re-state about her reaction to the photo of the hourglass? _____

   _____

   _____

   _____

   _____

Blueprint Reaction Essay 2: A Reaction to Dylan Thomas' "Do Not Go Gentle into that Good Night"

PREREADING DISCUSSION QUESTIONS

   1. Do you enjoy reading poetry?

   2. What are your feelings about death? Do you accept it easily? Are you afraid of it?

READING AND ANSWERING QUESTIONS

Read the following poem and essay. Then answer the questions.

DO NOT GO GENTLE INTO THAT GOOD NIGHT
by Dylan Thomas

Dylan Thomas

Do not go gentle into that
   good night,
Old age should burn and
   rave at close of day;
Rage, rage against the dying
   of the light.

Though wise men at their end know dark is right,
Because their words had forked no lightning they
Do not go gentle into that good night.

Good men, the last wave by, crying how bright
Their frail deeds might have danced in a green bay,
Rage, rage against the dying of the light.

Wild men who caught and sang the sun in flight,
And learn, too late, they grieved it on its way,
Do not go gentle into that good night.

Grave men, near death, who see with blinding sight
Blind eyes could blaze like meteors and be gay,
Rage, rage against the dying of the light.

And you, my father, there on the sad height,
Curse, bless, me now with your fierce tears, I pray.
Do not go gentle into that good night.
Rage, rage against the dying of the light.

by Dylan Thomas, from THE POEMS OF DYLAN
THOMAS, copyright © 1952 by Dylan Thomas.
Reprinted by permission of New Directions
Publishing Corp.

A REACTION TO DYLAN THOMAS' "DO NOT GO GENTLE INTO THAT GOOD NIGHT"

1   One of the most well-known poems by Dylan Thomas is "Do Not Go Gentle into that Good Night." Thomas' father had been suffering from throat cancer, and Thomas wrote this poem on the eve of his father's death. "Do Not Go Gentle into that Good Night" is the cry of a man who does not want to see his father die. In the six stanzas of the poem, Thomas examines how different types of people deal with death. He explains their struggles and at the same asks his father to fight death. Thomas' poem is a testament to struggle and a plea to his father not to give in to death. In reading this poem, my feeling is that all people should fight against the **inevitability** of death.

(continued)

inevitability:
impossibility of
avoiding or
preventing

(continued)

2   Thomas writes that wise men who know that they will experience death fight it. They are aware of the **futility** of trying to continue living, but they attempt to hold on to life. I believe this fight occurs because they feel that they have not done enough good deeds yet. These wise men want to contribute more to society, but death will take them **regardless** of their battle to **circumvent** it.

3   Good, simple men are also known to battle death. Their lives have probably been **uneventful** compared to the lives of the wise men who spent their lives teaching others. However, neither do these people accept death so **readily.** How often do we hear of an average person, a hardworking soul, who struggles to the bitter end of a long illness? It is these common men who routinely show their strength at the end of their lives, but they never win the battle in the end.

4   The third group of men mentioned in the poem is wild men with courage to do and try things that others cannot or will not do. In my opinion, these are the people who fight against death the hardest. Adventurers like these often do not realize their own **mortality.** In these cases, I believe the shock of death in a wild man's eyes is much stronger than in others'.

5   Thomas also includes grave men who battle against death. The serious people who go about their lives without experiencing much pleasure do not want to die. I find this ironic, for why would serious or critical people, perhaps unhappy, want to continue living? These are the souls who are most likely to anticipate death, not fight it. However, Thomas includes them here with all other people who come to a realization before death that they do not want to leave this earth.

6   Death is something that all of us must confront sooner or later. In "Do Not Go Gentle into that Good Night," Dylan Thomas is reminding us that it is human nature to fight the inevitable. Death does not **discriminate** against anyone, yet the human reaction to it is mainly one of resistance.

futility: hopelessness

regardless: despite; anyway
circumvent: avoid

uneventful: unimportant; boring

readily: easily; willingly

mortality: death; fatality

discriminate: see clear differences

POSTREADING QUESTIONS

1. Reread the introductory paragraph. What background method is used to introduce the material? Summarize .

2. What is the thesis statement of this essay? Write it here. _____

_____

3. What is the general topic of this essay? _____

_____

4. *The controlling idea of a topic sentence is the idea that will be discussed in the paragraph. Write the controlling idea in each body paragraph.*

   a. _____

   b. _____

   c. _____

   d. _____

5. *Synonyms are often used in essays to enhance coherence. Read the vocabulary words in the chart. Refer to the essay and fill in the synonym column.*

Vocabulary word	Synonym
(paragraph 2) fight	battle
(paragraph 3) battle	st
(paragraph 5) grave	serious

6. *Pronouns are also used to add coherence. Reread paragraph 2. Circle the pronouns that refer to "wise men." Underline the pronouns that refer to the word "death."*

7. *Read the concluding paragraph. What is the author's final opinion about the poem?*

   _____

   _____

   _____

   _____

   _____

Grammar Focus and Sentence Check

Grammar Focus: Word Forms

The most common parts of speech in English are *nouns, verbs, adjectives,* and *adverbs.* As you learn vocabulary and practice its variations, or word forms, you will advance your writing that much more.

1. *Nouns.* A noun is a person, place, thing, or idea. Some examples are *father, shore, computer, generosity.* Many words can be made into nouns by adding a suffix. A list of common noun suffixes follows.

   -ance, -ence, -or, -er, -ee, -ist, -ism, -ship, -tion, -sion, -ness, -hood, -dom, -ity, -ian

   Examples: Coopera*tion* in the neighbor*hood* for crime watch was at an all-time high.

   Two of our local politi*cians* were recently accused of embezzling funds.

2. *Verbs.* A verb is any type of action or state of being, such as *jump* and *be.*

   Here are some common verb suffixes.

   -ify, -ize, -en, -ate

   Examples: In order to height*en* his awareness of literature, Bob initi*ated* a literature club at his high school.

   The media tends to politic*ize* many events, even if they are not necessarily political in nature.

3. *Adjectives.* An adjective modifies a noun. Typical adjective suffixes include:

   -able, -ible, -al, -tial, -ful, -ous, -tive, -less, -some, -ish

   Examples: Lisa's child*ish* prank in the classroom made her teacher furi*ous.*

   The politic*al* activists were arrested last weekend during the protest march.

4. *Adverbs.* An adverb *modifies* a verb or an adjective. Many adverbs are formed by adding *–ly* to an adjective.

   Examples: Bryant sang wonderful*ly* at the concert last night.

   Personally, Brendan Svenson is a fine man; political*ly,* he doesn't have the experience to succeed in office.

EXERCISE

6

FINDING WORD FORMS IN ESSAYS

Study the word forms below. Refer to Blueprint essay 1 (p. 150) and Blueprint essay 2 (pp. 152–153) to find the missing word forms. The first one is done for you.

NOUN	VERB	ADJECTIVE	ADVERB
Blueprint essay 1			
1. simplicity	simplify	*simple*	simply
2. persistence	persist	persistent	Persistently
3. History	x	historical	historically
4. Creator	create	creative	creatively
5. appreciation	appreciate	appreciative	x
6. smoothness	smooth	smooth	Smothlly
7. purity	purify	Pure	purely
Blueprint essay 2			
8. logic	x	logical	logically
9. death	die	dead/deadly	x
10. Inevitability	x	inevitable	inevitably
11. Streng	strengthen	strong	strongly
12. Pleasure	please	pleasant	pleasantly
13. irony	x	Ironic	ironically
14. reality	realize	real	really
15. critic/criticism	criticize	Critical	critically
16. discrimination	discriminate	discriminating/ed	x

Sentence Check: Sentence Variety

To write a well-crafted essay, good writers use sentence variety. There are four main ways to create sentence variety: *coordination, subordination, use of relative pronouns in subordination,* and *use of prepositional phrases.*

1. *Coordination.* Coordination connects two sets of ideas (clauses, sentences, or phrases) using these coordinating conjunctions: *and, but, or, nor, yet, for,* and *so.*

   Original sentences: The firefighters arrived on the scene in only five minutes. The fire was out of control by that time.

   Combined sentence: The firefighters arrived on the scene in only five minutes, **but** the fire was out of control by that time.

2. *Subordination.* Subordination links two sentences that are related. One of the sentences is the main idea, or independent clause, and the other takes on a subordinate (minor) role. Some common connectors used for subordination are: *after, because, before, even if, if, since, though, until, when, while, where.*

   Original sentences: The economic summit was postponed. Three key players could not attend.

   Combined sentence: The economic summit was postponed **because** three key players could not attend.

3. *Use of Relative Pronouns in Subordination.* Relative pronouns combine two clauses into one sentence. The subordinate clause begins with a relative pronoun and describes the independent clause. Common relative pronouns are *which, who, whoever, whom, that, whose.*

   Original sentences: My uncle owns a fine dining restaurant. The restaurant is always full.

   Combined sentence: My uncle owns a fine dining restaurant **that** is always full.

4. *Use of Prepositional Phrases.* A prepositional phrase adds information to the sentence. Some prepositions are *in, on, from, for, with, among, to, at.*

   Original sentences: We heard a frightening noise. The noise came from the attic.

   Combined sentence: We heard a frightening noise **from** the attic.

EXERCISE

7

SENTENCE VARIETY

Read the excerpts from Blueprint essay 1 (p. 150) and Blueprint essay 2 (pp. 152–153). Underline and label the sentence variety elements that occur in each excerpt: coordination (C), subordination (S), relative pronouns (RP), and prepositional phrases (PP). (Hint: Look for at least two examples in each excerpt.) The first one is done for you.

                     C   PP

1. Time is passing, <u>and</u> I can see it. It is right there <u>in front of</u> me.

2. I cannot lie <u>to</u> myself and tell myself <u>that</u> I will do what I need <u>to do</u>
           PP   RP   PP

   tomorrow or the next day.

3. I had better hurry up and do something <u>with</u> my life <u>before</u> the grains
                                       PP   S

   <u>of</u> sand have all fallen <u>through</u> the crevice.
   PP

4. The poem is the cry <u>of</u> a man <u>who</u> does not want to see his father die.
                           PP   RP

5. This fight occurs <u>because</u> they feel <u>that</u> they have not done enough
                     S   RP

   good deeds yet. These wise men want to contribute more, <u>but</u> death
                                                                C

   will take them anyway.

EDITING PRACTICE: GRAMMAR FOCUS AND SENTENCE CHECK APPLICATION

EXERCISE

8

Read this paragraph carefully. Find and correct the six errors in word forms. The first one is done for you.

Whenever I see a store window decorated with Christmas trees and Santa Claus, I experience a variety of feelings. The first emotion that comes to me is one of ~~happy~~ *happiness*. This time of year, especially in my country, is filled with love, ~~joyful~~ *joy*, and hope for the future. People seem friendlier and more ~~kindness~~ *Kindner*. This emotion, however, sometimes gives way to another more negative one. I feel disgusted, cheated, and materialistic. By letting myself get caught up in the frenetic rush to spend money, I ~~cheap~~ *cheat* the holiday itself. I wish I could ignore the ads and go with my ~~feel~~ *feeling*, to be ~~closely~~ *close* with my family and enjoy this season. Maybe it will happen next year.

The Writing Process: Practice Writing a Reaction Essay

Objectives

Prewriting:

Planning:

Partner Feedback:

First Draft:

Partner Feedback:

Final Draft:

In Part B, you will:

use your eyes "as a camera"

combine descriptions and reactions in a chart

review classmates' charts and analyze feedback

write a reaction essay
use background information in the essay

review classmates' essays and analyze feedback

use feedback to write a final draft of your reaction essay

The Writing Process: Writing Assignment

Your assignment is to write a reaction to a photo. Study the photo below. What do you see? How does it make you feel? Does it remind you of anything you have seen in real life or in your field of study? Follow the steps in the writing process in this section.

This Camera is an amazing object to capture moments in Color, brightness and with the better lends. Olympus is the best brand of cameras with the a memory of 620gb to record everything you want.

Prewriting: Using Your Eyes as a Camera

When you react to a visual prompt, you need to convey to the reader a strong impression of what you are looking at, so it is important to begin with a vivid description. By focusing on description, you not only brainstorm information to put in the background of the essay, but you also get a feeling for the reaction you will produce in the rest of the essay.

DESCRIBING IMAGES

Imagine that your eyes are a wandering camera. Look at all aspects of the photo on p. 159. How many images do you see? How is the lighting in the photo? What are the textures? What actions are happening? Fill in the chart below.

WHAT DO YOU SEE?

Object	Description	Actions	Light	Texture
Bad houses				
Tables				
Trash				
dirty clothes				
Bottles of water contaminated				
Broken floor				

EXERCISE
10

GENERATING PERSONAL REACTION

1. Based on the descriptions you noted in the chart in Exercise 8 and a review of the photo on p. 159, summarize your main reaction in a sentence or two.

_____

_____

2. Now break down your main reaction into three or four smaller, related feelings. Fill in the blanks in the chart. Keep referring back to the photo on p. 159 as you work.

Emotion 1	
Emotion 2	
Emotion 3	
Emotion 4	

EXERCISE
11

BRAINSTORMING SUPPORTING INFORMATION

In **column 1** *below, write each of the emotions you wrote in Exercise 10. Then fill in* **column 2** *with words and ideas that explain or relate to the emotion. You will use this information as supporting details in your body paragraphs.*

Emotions	Details
1.	
2.	
3.	
4.	

Planning: Combining Descriptions and Reactions

Now that you have described the illustration and explained your feelings about it, you are ready to plan how all this information will appear in an essay. Begin with description, then organize the body paragraphs, each dealing with one emotion. Use the chart to organize your essay.

EXERCISE

12

CHARTING YOUR ESSAY INFORMATION

Combine the information you generated in Exercises 9, 10, and 11 into the chart below and add introductory and concluding information. Except for the thesis statement, you do not have to write complete sentences. Follow these steps.

1. For the introductory paragraph, add some descriptive notes about the photo.

2. Write a thesis statement that tells your main reaction to the photo and indicates what you will discuss in the essay.

3. Choose the emotions that you will discuss in each body paragraph. What supporting details will you include?

4. Write notes about a final, summarizing opinion of the photo.

Introductory description	
Thesis statement	
Body paragraphs	1. 2. 3.
Concluding ideas	

Partner Feedback Form 1

Exchange outlines with another student. Read your partner's outline and answer the questions on Partner Feedback Form 1: Unit 6, p. 239, in Appendix 3. Discuss your partner's reactions to your outline. Make notes about any parts you need to change before you write your paper. For more information about giving partner feedback, see Appendix 2, p. 218, Guidelines for Partner Feedback.

First Draft

You are now ready to write the first draft of your essay. Before you begin, review your chart from Exercise 12 and any comments from your partner.

EXERCISE

13

WRITING THE INTRODUCTION

Write an introduction for your topic, using your chart and the feedback you received from your partner. Use description as background information in your introduction to begin your essay (see p. 147). "The Hourglass and Me" on p. 150 uses this type of introductory information. You can use it as a model if you want. End your introduction with a well-constructed thesis statement. When you finish, use the checklist to review your work.

Introduction Checklist

	YES	NO
► Did I use effective background information in the form of description?	☐	☐
► Do I avoid writing my personal reaction to the illustration in my introduction—waiting until the thesis?	☐	☐
► Does my thesis statement provide the reader with a clear guide that the essay will discuss my reaction to the illustration?	☐	☐
► Is the purpose of my essay clear?	☐	☐

What is it? _____

EXERCISE

14

WRITING BODY PARAGRAPHS

*Look again at your introductory paragraph and the **charts** you created to plan your reaction essay. Then write the body paragraphs. When you finish, use the checklist to review your work.*

(!)

IMPORTANT NOTE:

One important thing to consider when you write a reaction essay is to use personal feelings in your body paragraphs. In this type of writing, it is appropriate to use the first person singular, *I*.

Body Paragraph Checklist

	YES	NO
► Does each body paragraph treat only one main emotion or reaction?	☐	☐
► Does each contain a topic sentence with a clear controlling idea?	☐	☐
► Does each paragraph end with a logical concluding sentence?	☐	☐
► Do my body paragraphs all relate to and support the thesis statement of the essay? In other words, does each address part of my reaction?	☐	☐
► Do I repeat important key terms?	☐	☐

(continued)

Body Paragraph Checklist (continued)

	YES	NO
▸ Do I use pronouns to help my writing flow coherently?	☐	☐
▸ Do I use synonyms for key words in my body paragraphs?	☐	☐
▸ Are all the word forms correct?	☐	☐
▸ Do I use sentence variety?	☐	☐
▸ Are all sentences in my body paragraphs relevant to the topic? That is, do they have unity?	☐	☐

EXERCISE

15

WRITING A CONCLUSION

Review again your chart, introduction, and body. Write a concluding paragraph for your essay. When you finish, use the checklist to review your work.

Conclusion Checklist

	YES	NO
▸ Does my conclusion successfully signal the end of my essay?	☐	☐
▸ Does my conclusion add coherence to the essay by:		
a. restating the essay thesis?	☐	☐
b. summarizing or restating the essay subtopics?	☐	☐
▸ Does my conclusion:		
a. leave the reader with my final thoughts?	☐	☐
b. offer a final, summarizing opinion about my reaction to the illustration?	☐	☐

Partner Feedback Form 2

Exchange essays with another student. Read your partner's essay and answer the questions on Partner Feedback Form 2: Unit 6, pp. 241–242, in Appendix 3. Discuss your partner's reactions to your essay. Make notes about any parts you need to change before you write your second draft. For more information about giving partner feedback, see Appendix 2, p. 218, Guidelines for Partner Feedback.

Final Draft

Carefully revise your essay using all the feedback you have received: partner review of your chart and essay, instructor comments, and any evaluation you have done yourself. Use the checklist to do a final check of your essay. In addition, try reading your essay aloud. This can help you find awkward-sounding sentences and errors in punctuation. When you finish, add a title to your essay and neatly type your final draft. See Appendix 4, p. 246, for information about writing titles.

Final Draft Checklist

	YES	NO
▶ Did I use an effective description to introduce the illustration I am reacting to?	☐	☐
▶ Did I include a thesis statement that contains a clear topic and controlling idea?	☐	☐
▶ Did I focus my reaction on my feelings and thoughts?	☐	☐
▶ Did I use the first person "I" in my body paragraphs to explain my reaction?	☐	☐
▶ Did I create coherence by		
a. repeating key nouns in my body paragraphs?	☐	☐
b. replacing some nouns with pronouns?	☐	☐
c. using synonyms for some key vocabulary to avoid sounding repetitive?	☐	☐
▶ Have I used sentence variety and correct word forms?	☐	☐
▶ Are all my topic sentences clear and focused?	☐	☐
▶ Does my concluding paragraph successfully signal the end of my essay and sound like a final paragraph?	☐	☐
▶ Does my essay have unity and coherence?	☐	☐

Additional Writing Assignments from the Academic Disciplines

Beginning with the Prewriting activity on p. 160, use the writing process and write another essay. Choose a topic from the following list.

SUBJECT

WRITING TASK

Entertainment

Write a reaction essay about a film you have recently seen. Summarize the film's plot in the introduction. How did you feel about the film? Could you identify with the situation? How do you evaluate the film?

Politics

Write a reaction to the concept of Marxism. First summarize or explain Marxism, then react to it as a concept. What does it mean to you? Do you agree with its philosophy? Why or why not?

Literature

Write a reaction essay about a short story. In the introductory paragraph, summarize the plot of the story. How does the story relate to your life? What are your feelings about what you read? What significance does the story have for you?

Lecture Analysis

Write a reaction to a lecture you have recently attended. Include a brief summary. What did you know about the topic prior to listening to the lecture? How does your experience add to the information you learned? What is your reaction to the topic and the instructor's delivery style?

Blueprints for

ARGUMENTATIVE ESSAYS

Blueprints for Argumentative Essays

Objectives	In Part A, you will:
Analysis:	study the structure of argumentative essays
Unity and Coherence:	
Unity:	learn how to take only one stance
Coherence: Transition Expressions	learn to use *although it may be true that/despite the fact that, certainly,* and *surely*
Grammar Focus:	study prepositions
Sentence Check:	study noun clauses
Practice:	determine the opposing sides of an issue and use different methods of organization

IMPORTANT NOTE:

Often argumentative essays include some of the other types of writing discussed in *Blueprints*. For example, you may want to *compare and contrast* (Unit 4) the opposing views in your essay to show the reader why your view is the best one. Or, to illustrate your point that a diet low in cholesterol can prevent heart disease, you might explain the *process* (Unit 3) of how cholesterol develops into plaque in coronary arteries. You will study more about using these and other methods later in this unit.

What Is an Argumentative Essay?

Writers choose argumentative essays when they want to persuade readers to change their minds about something. In this kind of essay, writers must convince readers of their point of view.

Developing an Argumentative Essay

The word "issue" is frequently used to describe a problem situation in which there are differing points of view. To argue about an issue, you must first discover all the different sides of the issue and which viewpoints you agree with. Then, you must clearly understand *what the opposing viewpoint is.* It is helpful to first state your viewpoint in a direct and clear manner. Then take the opposite position: what is that viewpoint? Stating the opposing viewpoint will help you clearly identify an opponent's position, which you will need to address in your essay.

EXERCISE

1

DETERMINING THE OPPOSING VIEWPOINTS

Determine the opposing viewpoints for each of the following statements. Write the viewpoints in the blanks. The first one is done for you.

1. Early childhood education programs prevent later criminal activity.

   Early childhood education programs have no impact on later criminal activity.

2. Parents should impose rules for their teenage children about the use of the Internet.

   Teenagers don't need imposed rules for their parenst to use internet

3. Doctors and nurses do not provide adequate pain management for terminally ill patients.

   _____

   _____

4. Marijuana use for medical purposes should not be legalized in the United States.

   _____

   _____

5. It is perfectly ethical to accept donations from pharmaceutical companies to conduct scientific research at universities.

   _____

   _____

Once you choose a side to defend and state the opposite argument, you can develop your argument by *creating a list of reasons for your viewpoint.*

EXERCISE

SUPPORTING IDEAS

For each main argument, think of two different supporting ideas to back it up. Write your ideas after each statement. The first one is done for you.

1. Columbus Day should not be celebrated as a holiday in the United States.

   a. *Columbus did not really "discover" America.*

   b. *Columbus slaughtered and enslaved native people.*

2. Spanking is harmful to children.

a. _____

b. _____

3. A vegetarian diet is healthier than one that includes meat.

a. _____

b. _____

4. One parent should care for children full time until they begin school.

a. _____

b. _____

5. The government should not prevent genetic cloning of human organs for medical purposes.

a. _____

b. _____

Introductions in Argumentative Essays

To begin your argumentative essay, you can use any of the introductory techniques already presented in *Blueprints 2,* including turning an argument on its head (explained in Unit 1, p. 17, and later in this unit on page 195). No matter which technique you use, your first paragraph needs to include the following:

▶ a brief explanation of the issue (This can include background information to help the reader understand what the topic is all about.)

▶ a clear statement of both sides of the issue

▶ an argumentative thesis statement, which is distinctive in that it takes a stand on the issue

Methods of Organization for Argumentative Essays

There are three common methods of organizing an argumentative essay. No one method is better than another; each one provides a different way of organizing the details of your argument and countering the opposing viewpoint. What is important to know is that following any one of these methods of organization will provide order and logic to your essay. Review the chart below. Note that you may have more or fewer details and arguments in your essay than you see here.

Method 1	**Method 2**	**Method 3**

1. Introduction
  a. Explanation of the issue (Use an introductory technique, such as turning an argument on its head.)
  b. Statement of both sides of the issue
  c. Argumentative thesis statement
 	
2. Argument 1 for your stance
  a. Detail 1
  b. Detail 2
  c. Etc.
 	
3. Argument 2 for your stance
  a. Detail 1
  b. Detail 2
  c. Etc.
 	
4. Argument 3 for your stance
  a. Detail 1
  b. Detail 2
  c. Etc.
 	
5. Counter-argument
  a. Statement of the opposing view
  b. Refutation of opposing view 1
  c. Refutation of opposing view 2
  d. Etc.
 	
6. Conclusion
  a. Detail 1
  b. Detail 2
  c. Etc.
	1. Introduction
	  a. Explanation of the issue (Use an introductory technique, such as turning an argument on its head.)
	  b. Statement of both sides of the issue
	  c. Argumentative thesis statement
	
	2. Refute the opposing stance with Argument 1
	  a. Statement of the opposing stance
	  b. Detail 1
	  c. Detail 2
	  d. Etc.
	
	3. Refute the opposing stance with Argument 2
	  a. Detail 1
	  b. Detail 2
	  c. Etc.
	
	4. Refute the opposing stance with Argument 3
	  a. Detail 1
	  b. Detail 2
	  c. Etc.
	
	5. Conclusion
	  a. Detail 1
	  b. Detail 2
	  c. Etc.
		1. Introduction
		  a. Explanation of the issue (Use an introductory technique, such as turning an argument on its head.)
		  b. Statement of both sides of the issue
		  c. Argumentative thesis statement
		
		2. Counter-argument
		  a. Statement of the opposing view
		  b. Refutation of opposing view 1
		  c. Refutation of opposing view 2
		  d. Etc.
		
		3. Argument 1 for your stance (weakest)
		  a. Detail 1
		  b. Detail 2
		  c. Etc.
		
		4. Argument 2 for your stance (stronger)
		  a. Detail 1
		  b. Detail 2
		  c. Etc.
		
		5. Argument 3 for your stance (strongest)
		  a. Detail 1
		  b. Detail 2
		  c. Etc.
		
		6. Conclusion
		  a. Detail 1
		  b. Detail 2
		  c. Etc.

Unity in Argumentative Essays

While you may understand more than one viewpoint about an issue, it is important to argue for only one viewpoint in your essay. Otherwise you might weaken your argument and your essay will lack unity. For example, you can confuse your reader if you stray from one position. You might even lend credibility to other views if you don't stay focused on one viewpoint.

Taking only one stance (viewpoint) in an argument helps you achieve **unity.** For example, if you argue against the death penalty but then assert that it is acceptable in some cases, you provide an opening for those who would argue for it in many more circumstances. This opposing viewpoint would discredit your argument (See Unit 1, pp. 4–5 and 21–22 for more about unity in essays.)

EXERCISE

3

STICKING TO ONE STANCE

One of the supporting statements listed for each viewpoint does not relate to the argument. Cross out the statement that does not belong in the list. The first one is done for you.

1. Television adversely affects children.

   a. Children who watch longs hours of television do not read often enough.

   b. School performance goes down when children spend many hours watching television

   ~~c. Some educational television programs help children who are visually oriented learn better.~~

2. The mounting body of science proving that manmade greenhouse gases trap heat in the earth's atmosphere is convincing more and more people that we must cut greenhouse pollution drastically.

   a. Global warming in coastal states like Florida will lead to flooding and saltwater contamination of underground drinking water supplies.

   b. More frequent wildfires and declining crop yields are only two of the consequences of global warming.

   (c.) This paper seeks to assist policymakers and the public in better understanding the institutional resistance to efforts to curb →stop greenhouse pollution.

3. Exposure to the sun for long periods can cause skin cancer.

   a. There is a direct connection between skin cancer and chronic exposure to the sun.

   b. A history of sunburns is correlated with skin cancer later in life.

   (c.) Exposure to sunlight is an important source of Vitamin D, a vital nutrient.

4. Alexander the Great was considered one of the finest kings of the western world.

   (a.) Although he brutally conquered many people, Alexander often encouraged the intermarriage of his own Macedonians and the women who survived his conquests.

    b. Alexander opened routes for trade and communication between the eastern and western worlds.

    c. Alexander's religious tolerance earned him the respect of many people around the world.

5. The benefits of space exploration are worth the costs.

    a. As natural resources needed for human survival are depleted, new sources may be found on other planets and moons.

    b. Eventually, to alleviate overcrowding on Earth, humans will need to settle on other planets.

    c. Most of our knowledge of the solar system comes from ground-based observations and Earth-orbiting satellites.

Coherence in Argumentative Essays

As discussed in previous units, the use of well-placed transition expressions is among the most important practices for adding coherence to paragraphs and essays. In addition to the transition expressions you have already learned, the ones below are especially useful for argumentative writing.

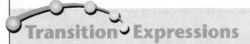

Transition Expressions

Transition Expressions: *although it may be true that/despite the fact that, certainly,* and *surely*

although it may be true that/despite the fact that

Function: to say that something is true before saying something else about it

Use: *Although it may be true that* and *despite that* are used to concede a point that supports the opposing argument. These transition expressions are followed by a clause that introduces the opposing view.

Examples: **Although it may be true that** there appear to be dry riverbeds on the planet Mars, this does not prove that water or life once existed there.

Despite the fact that the shortest distance between two points is a straight line, you cannot often drive or walk in a straight line to your destination.

Punctuation Note: *Although it may be true that/despite the fact that* + clause that states the opposing view is followed by a comma before stating your stance in a separate clause.

(continued)

(continued)

certainly

> **Function:** to say that the writer agrees with something without any doubt
>
> **Use:** *Certainly* is an adverb used in argumentative writing to lend credibility to the writer's stance.
>
> *Examples:* **Certainly** one would not wish to risk the lives of innocent people by driving recklessly.
>
> The new regime will **certainly** take over the formerly private industry to make it publicly controlled.

surely

> **Function:** implies that the writer has faith in the statement that follows
>
> **Use:** *Surely* is an adverb used to express certainty. It differs slightly from *certainly* in that *surely* expresses more urgency and persuasion.
>
> *Examples:* **Surely** if the banks run into trouble, the Federal Reserve should lower interest rates again.
>
> Nuclear power plants **surely** represent the most efficient energy sources for today's needs.

Blueprints Argumentative Essays

In this section, you will read and analyze two sample argumentative essays. These essays can act as blueprints when you write your own argumentative essay in Part B.

Blueprint Argumentative Essay 1: Why Adopt a Vegetarian Diet?

PREREADING DISCUSSION QUESTIONS

1. *Do you know anyone who is a vegetarian? Do you know why that person is a vegetarian?*

2. *Why do you think most vegetarians choose not to eat meat?*

EXERCISE

4

READING AND ANSWERING QUESTIONS

Read the argumentative essay. Fill in the blanks with transition expressions from the list. Then answer the postreading questions.

although it may be true that   surely   certainly

ingrained:
thoroughly filled, as
with an idea in the
mind

ethical: behaving
within accepted
boundaries of right
and wrong

adequate: enough
to satisfy a
requirement or need

consumption: the
act of eating or
drinking

erosion: a process
by which material is
worn away from the
earth's surface

organic waste:
undigested food
residue from living
animals

WHY ADOPT A VEGETARIAN DIET?

1   "Meat and potatoes" is a phrase used in American English that means the centerpiece of a meal. Besides referring to food, "meat" signifies the most important part of anything. It has been such a deeply **ingrained,** time-honored tradition for families to build a meal around meat, that one can safely say that meat has become the heart of an American meal. Meat gives us protein, and therefore, our strength. However, this widely held belief that meat is necessary for health and vitality has outlived its usefulness. While some people continue to hold onto this outdated perception of the importance of meat, others are letting go of it and becoming vegetarian. That is, Americans are correcting their beliefs about meat and increasingly becoming vegetarian for **ethical,** environmental, and health reasons.

2   One reason for becoming vegetarian is to prevent cruelty to animals. Animals, like humans, feel pain, stress, and fear. People cannot morally justify the pain and suffering of animals that are killed for food when **adequate** nutrition can be found in plant foods. Not only do animals experience these physical sensations when they are needlessly slaughtered for human **consumption,** but they are often treated cruelly prior to slaughter. Veal calves, for example, are forced to live in extremely small cages no longer than their bodies so they cannot move and create unwanted muscle. They are then killed when they are just twelve to sixteen weeks old so that their weak, immature muscles will produce soft meat.

3   In addition to ethical reasons, some vegetarians choose not to eat meat for environmental reasons. Cattle production, for example, is a major cause of soil **erosion** due to overgrazing of land, which creates deserts out of grasslands. Cattle production also creates water pollution through **organic waste** and the use of chemicals in animal feed. In addition, cattle production pollutes the air. Grain-fed cattle contribute significantly to global warming through the production of carbon dioxide, methane,

(continued)

(continued)

and nitrous oxide. The burning of the world's forests for cattle pasture has released billions of tons of carbon dioxide into the **atmosphere.** The world's cattle release millions of tons of methane through their digestive systems directly into the atmosphere each year. Moreover, producing feed crops for cattle involves the use of petro-chemical fertilizers, which **emit** vast amounts of nitrous oxide. These gases are building up in the atmosphere, blocking heat from escaping the planet, and could cause **cataclysmic** global climate changes in this century.

4   While some vegetarians make the choice not to eat meat for ethical and environmental reasons, others are concerned with personal health. The health benefits of not eating meat are undisputed, even among the most traditional and conservative medical doctors today. In scientific studies, vegetarian diets are **correlated** with lower **cholesterol** levels, lower rates of heart disease, high blood pressure, obesity, diabetes, and colon cancer. As a result, vegetarians tend to live longer, healthier lives.

5   Some fear that not eating meat will be difficult for nutritional, cultural, and practical reasons, but these fears can be easily **allayed.** Because meat, poultry, or fish is traditionally the focal point of meals, some people think meals are inadequate without a large portion of protein on the table, with vegetables downgraded to secondary roles. _____ most meat-eating Americans get the bulk of their iron, protein, and vitamin B12 from meat sources, people can easily get **ample** amounts of these nutrients from a varied diet that includes nuts, seeds, and grains. Even vegans, who eat no animal products at all, can take a daily vitamin and mineral supplement to bolster iron and vitamin B12 intake. Most restaurants now cater to vegetarians, especially ethnic restaurants like Mexican, Italian, and Indian, making it easy to be vegetarian and eat out. Even when there are no vegetarian choices on the menu, most chefs will _____ be happy to **oblige** when asked to produce a special vegetarian meal. Finally, when faced with family food traditions that involve meat eating,

atmosphere: the mass of gas surrounding a planet, especially Earth

emit: to give or send out matter or energy

cataclysmic: causing a violent upheaval with great destruction

correlated: related in a parallel or interchangeable way

cholesterol: a white crystalline substance, $C_{27}H_{45}HO$; part of what makes cell membranes fluid

allayed: reduced the intensity of; calmed

ample: more than enough, fully sufficient for a purpose

oblige: to do a service or favor for

(continued)

(continued)

such as Thanksgiving, most vegetarians can ask the cook for a nonmeat choice ahead of time or may bring a vegetable dish of their own.

6   For most vegetarians, the choice to become vegetarian is not taken lightly. _____, if one was not brought up as a child to abstain from eating meat, the switch to vegetarianism means a change in deeply ingrained eating habits. The benefits of vegetarianism to animals, to the environment, and most of all to personal health, however, far outweigh the small inconvenience people might feel for a week or so after beginning a nonmeat diet. For all vegetarians, eating a flesh-free diet is a decision made for important global or personal reasons that not only impact personal health and well being, but also the health and well being of the planet. In the not-too-distant future, the phrase "meat and potatoes" will become a relic of the past, just like the **antiquated** belief in the need for a carnivorous diet.

antiquated: old-fashioned; out of date

Some parts adapted from http://www.mcspotlight.org/media/reports/beyond.html—
April 24, 2001

POSTREADING DISCUSSION QUESTIONS

1. *What is the thesis statement of this essay? Write it here.*

   _____

2. *What introduction technique is used in this essay? (See Unit 1, pp. 15–17 for a list of introductory techniques.)*

   Quotation

3. *What method of organization is used in this essay? (See Methods of Organization for Argumentative Essays on p. 171)*

   Method 1

4. *What point is the writer arguing in this essay?*

   Vegetarian diet

5. *What point of view is the opposite of what the writer is saying?*

   _____

6. *Write down each reason the writer gives to support the argument.*

   Reason 1: ___Ethical_____

   Reason 2: ___Enviromental_____

   Reason 3: ___health_____

7. *In an argumentative essay, the writer must address the viewpoint of the opposing argument. List the three opposing points that are taken up in this essay.*

   Point 1: ___nutitional_____

   Point 2: ___Cultural_____

   Point 3: ___Practical_____

8. *Underline the controlling idea of each body paragraph in the essay. Does each body paragraph address only one of the subtopics?*

   _____

9. *Does the writer convince you of his viewpoint?* ___Yes_____
   If not, why not?

   _____

10. *Does the conclusion provide a summary of the main points of the*

    argument? _____Yes_____

Blueprint Argumentative Essay 2: Coffee: Surprising Benefits from This Herbal Supplement

PREREADING DISCUSSION QUESTIONS

1. *Have you ever drunk coffee to stay up late to write a paper?*

2. *Do you think that coffee is good for you or bad for you? Why?*

3. *What are the benefits of drinking coffee? Are there any?*

4. *Do you think coffee has any medicinal value?*

READING AND ANSWERING QUESTIONS

Read the argumentative essay. Fill in the blanks with transition expressions from the list. Then answer the postreading questions.

surely   despite the fact that   certainly

COFFEE: SURPRISING BENEFITS FROM THIS HERBAL SUPPLEMENT

1 People everywhere are trying to cut back on their consumption of this "harmful" drink, all the while craving coffee desperately and feeling guilty when they indulge. Coffee is said to cause nervousness and is **purported** to be addictive. We have all heard about these harmful effects of coffee, but many Americans continue to drink it daily. What if instead of feeling guilty about drinking coffee, you could feel good about taking this herbal supplement? Consider these facts: coffee combats drowsiness, temporarily boosts athletic performance, eases congestion due to colds and flu, prevents asthma attacks, and **enhances** the pain-relieving effects of aspirin. Research on the benefits of coffee shows that it deserves our respect as an important supplement.

2 Over the years, many attempts have been made to associate coffee with negative health effects. However, these claims remain **unsubstantiated.** _____ coffee can cause sleeplessness and nervousness, this is true only when it is drunk in large doses. The medically important **constituent** of coffee is caffeine, but the caffeine content of coffee depends on how it is prepared. A cup of instant coffee contains about 60 milligrams of caffeine, whereas a cup of drip, percolated or even espresso coffee has about 100 milligrams. Most doctors say that coffee appears to pose no particular threat to most people if it is consumed in moderation. According to new research presented at the national meeting of the American Chemical Society, coffee is not very addictive. French researchers reported that caffeine has no effect on the area of the brain involved with addiction at doses of one to three cups of coffee per day. Astrid Nehlig, Ph.D. of the French National Health and Medical Research Institute conducted research on coffee consumption with laboratory animals. This research confirmed that while moderate does of caffeine contribute to increased alertness and energy, dependence does not occur at those levels.

(continued)

purported: given a false appearance

enhances: makes something greater or of more value

unsubstantiated: not established by proof or competent evidence

constituent: an essential part

(continued)

chlorogenic acid:
$C_{16}H_{18}O_9$, a substance that forms around infected tissue in some higher plants and has anti-fungal properties

cognition: mental ability

bronchodilator: a substance that causes expansion of the air spaces of the lungs

therapeutic: acting as a cure or relief

3 _____ coffee is best known as the powerful stimulant that helps people stay awake during night driving and cramming before final exams. Its caffeine is capable of boosting energy, increasing alertness, and quickening reaction time. It is also a mood elevator and may help mild depression. The explanation for this may lie in research conducted in the mid-1980s, which suggested that the **chlorogenic acids** in coffee might have an antidepressant effect on the opiate system in the brain. Recently, researchers from the University of Bristol reviewed a decade of research into caffeine's influence on **cognition** and mood. The survey revealed that a cup of coffee could help in the performance of tasks requiring sustained attention, even during low alertness situations such as after lunch, at night, or when a person has a cold.

4 Coffee's health advantages are not confined to mood elevation and increased energy; there are more specific benefits as well for colds, asthma, athletic performance and pain relief. Some over-the-counter cold formulas contain caffeine, partly to counteract the sedative effects of the antihistamines they contain, but caffeine also helps open the bronchial tubes, relieving the congestion of colds and flu. Coffee's action as a **bronchodilator** can also help prevent asthma attacks. In addition, several studies show that, compared with plain aspirin, the combination of aspirin and caffeine relieves pain significantly better than aspirin alone. The reason is caffeine's ability to speed up the body's metabolism so that the aspirin's pain reducing effects are felt faster. Finally, coffee may also improve physical stamina, according to a report published in the journal *The Physician and Sports Medicine.* Athletes who want coffee's benefits typically drink three or four cups during the hour or two before an event.

5 Although most people don't think of it as such, coffee is

_____Coffe is_____ America's most popular herbal beverage. Despite the scare tactics of those who would try to discredit coffee's reputation, years of research have not shown harmful effects, when coffee is taken in moderation. It not only helps a sleepy nation wake up in the morning, but it also has significant **therapeutic** value, which has been scientifically proven.

Adapted from http://www.healthyideas.com/healing/herb/coffee.html

Prevention magazine reports, and

http://www.accessexcellence.com/WN/SUA12/cafe399.html,

May 2001

POSTREADING DISCUSSION QUESTIONS

1. What is the argumentative thesis statement of this essay? Write it here.

    _____

2. How many subtopics are there? What are they? Write them here.

    _____

3. Does the introductory paragraph include background information about the issue?

    _____Yes_____

4. Does the introduction section include a clear statement of both sides of the issue?

    _____yes_____

5. Underline the controlling idea of each body paragraph in the essay. Does each body paragraph address one of the subtopics?

    _____

6. What one stance is taken on the issue to provide unity?

    _____

    Is the argument successful? _____

7. What is the opposing argument? _____

    _____

8. Which method of organization is used to develop the argument? (See Methods of Organization for Argumentative Essays on p. 171.)

    _____

9. An argumentative essay includes details about each reason offered to support the argument. Often the details are examples. At other times they might be details of a process, causes and effects, comparisons, etc. What is primarily used in this essay to give details about the reasons for the author's view? Circle one.

    examples   descriptions of a process

    causes and effects   comparisons

    the opinion of experts

10. Besides signaling the end of the essay, what other purpose does the conclusion fulfill?

    _____

Grammar Focus and Sentence Check

Grammar Focus: Prepositions

A **preposition** is a word that takes a noun or pronoun object. It often expresses meanings like time, location, or direction. A preposition plus its object is called a **prepositional phrase.**

Examples:

direction	**location**	**time**
to Bangkok	*in* the attic	*after* the storm

Prepositional phrases can occur in several positions in the sentence. Those that express the idea of time are found at the beginning or end of a sentence.

Examples:

During the evening, I stay away from the computer.

I stay away from the computer **during the evening.**

Prepositional phrases that show location or direction occur after the verb and the object of the verb.

Examples:

Cattle release methane **into the atmosphere.**

Students find articles **in scholarly journals.**

Some very common prepositional phrases usually occur with no article. They often refer to everyday activities like eating, sleeping, working, and studying.

at home	*in* school	*to* school
at school	*in* church	*to* church
at church	*in* bed	*to* lunch

Example:

Q: Where's Keith?

A: He's **at school.**

However, when the object of the preposition refers to a specific location (like the building itself), it occurs with an article.

Examples:

Q: Are you going to Keith's party? It's **at the community center.**

A: I'm going **to the community center,** but not **to the party.**

Common prepositional phrases referring to transportation also occur with no article:

by plane/train/car	*on* foot

Examples:

I went **by car,** but Lisa went **on foot.**

EXERCISE

6

PREPOSITIONAL PHRASES IN *COFFEE: SURPRISING BENEFITS FROM THIS HERBAL SUPPLEMENT*

Reread Blueprint essay 2, "Coffee: Surprising Benefits from This Herbal Supplement."

IMPORTANT NOTE:

Infinitives are often mistaken for prepositional phrases. An infinitive is *to* + **the base form of a verb** and functions as a noun.

Examples: Even vegans, who eat no animal products at all, can take a daily vitamin and mineral supplement **to bolster** iron and vitamin B12 intake.

Most doctors say that coffee appears **to pose** no particular threat to most people if it is consumed in moderation.

Prepositional phrases that use *to* often express direction or location.

Examples: The bill, with the chairman's approval, is going **to committee.**

Later, the Dutch brought the coffee plant **to Java.**

1. Underline all the prepositional phrases that you can find in this essay.

2. How many prepositional phrases did you find? _____

   Write them here. _____

   _____

   _____

   _____

   _____

   _____

   _____

   _____

   _____

   _____

EXERCISE

7

ARTICLE OR NO ARTICLE?

Decide whether an article is needed as part of the prepositional phrase in each sentence. Circle the correct prepositional phrase.

1. After class, Bill and Omi are going _____ in the cafeteria.

   a. to lunch   b. to the lunch

2. Masako's husband goes _____ after she leaves.

   a. to work   b. to the work

3. Harold is not _____ today.

   a. in school   b. in the school

4. He's sick, so he stayed home _____.

   a. in bed   b. to bed

5. Beth doesn't have a car. She goes everywhere _____.

   a. by the foot   b. on foot

PREPOSITIONAL PHRASES IN ARGUMENTATIVE ESSAYS

A. Specific prepositions and prepositional phrases can be used in different types of writing as you develop your argument. Study this chart:

Type of Writing	Use of Prepositional Phrases	Examples
Argumentative	To concede (admit) a point made by the opposition	Despite, in spite of + Noun Phrase
Comparison	To compare one thing or idea to another	like + Noun Phrase as + Noun Phrase
Process /Description	To explain the chronological order of events	<u>in</u>, on, at, <u>during</u>, by, <u>until</u>
	To explain the spatial order of things	in, around, from, through, out of

B. Write a preposition in each sentence, using the chart to assist you. Then, following each sentence, decide to which type of writing the sentence belongs. The first one is done for you.

1. <u>Like</u> Christmas, Chanukah is celebrated shortly before the beginning of the new year and involves lighting candles.

   Writing type: *comparison*

2. <u>In spite of</u> the warning signals that were sent out by the military, protestors continued their demonstration.

   Writing type: <u>Argumentative</u>

3. <u>During</u> the 1960s in the United States, laws that might have protected the civil rights of African Americans were often not enforced.

   Writing type: <u>Process</u>

4. _____*In*_____ the Cold War, much of the world was divided politically in terms of alliance with either the former Soviet Union or the United States.

   Writing type: _____

5. _____*X*_____ Marx, Comte, and Weber believed in the possibility of using scientific methods to study the behavior of people in groups.

   Writing type: _____

6. _____*Despite*_____ the fact that the Kyoto Protocol was not signed by the United States, there is still hope for an international response to global warming.

   Writing type: _____*Argumentative*_____

Sentence Check: Noun Clauses

Noun clauses function like nouns. Like all clauses, a noun clause has a subject and a verb. A noun clause can begin with *that,* a *wh-* word, *if,* or *whether.* These words link a noun clause to the main clause of the sentence.

Main Clause	Noun Clause
It is not certain	**if/whether vegetarianism will increase in popularity.**
They asked	**where Wallace is staying.**
I know	**that coffee helps me wake up in the morning.**

Functions and Rules for Noun Clauses

1. Noun clauses usually function like nouns: they can be subjects, subject complements, objects of verbs, and objects of prepositions. Note that as subjects, noun clauses take singular verbs.

   What you just saw is an incredible facsimile. (subject)

   Their belief is **that agriculture should provide shelter as well as food.** (subject complement)

   I don't know **whether they left yet or not.** (object)

   She looked around **where he lost his keys.** (object of preposition)

2. Noun clauses can also follow some adjectives, such as *certain* and *happy*.

Trang is certain **that the spring rolls are cooked.**

The golfers were happy **that the rain stopped.**

3. Noun clauses tend to be used with verbs and adjectives that express mental activity.

I *decided* **that I don't trust her.**

He is *positive* **that the door was locked.**

EXERCISE

9

IDENTIFYING NOUN CLAUSES

Underline the noun clauses in the following sentences. Then rewrite the sentences, substituting a different noun clause in the same place in the sentence. The first one is done for you.

1. Can you tell me <u>if this plane is going to Chicago</u>? *Can you tell me if the library will be open till 10:00 tonight?*

2. This video shows how coffee beans are processed.

_____

3. Whether accepting campaign contributions from oil companies is

ethical or not is the subject of the debate. _____

_____

4. Can you hear which song is playing on the radio right now?

_____

5. It doesn't surprise me that you passed the test.

_____

Noun Clauses with *That*

1. Noun clauses with *that* can be used after many verbs and adjectives. The word *that* is often omitted.

   Although it may be true **that the television is on,** Kevin has fallen asleep and is not watching it.

   I am sure **(that) the temperature has dropped.**

2. The word *that* cannot be omitted if the noun clause is in the subject position.

   ***That* you are a student** is news to me. **Not:** You are a student is news to me.

3. Although *that* clauses appear in the subject position, more often the word *it* is the subject.

   ***That* you are a student** is news to me. = **It** is news to me **that you are a student.**

4. Noun phrases like *the fact, the idea* and *the possibility* often precede *that* clauses.

   The possibility *that* we can affect global warming is astounding.

5. Noun clauses with *that* are used in reported speech. You use reported speech when you offer the opinions of experts in defending an argument.

   "The Kyoto Protocol is necessary to address the problem of global warming," said the world leader.

   The world leader said **that the Kyoto Protocol is necessary to address the problem of global warming.**

EXERCISE

10

CHANGING QUOTES TO REPORTED SPEECH WITH NOUN CLAUSES

Use the sentences with quotes to form new sentences with noun clauses beginning with that. *The first one is done for you*

1. "There has been an overemphasis in this conference about drugs," said an AIDS adviser for Save the Children.

   An AIDS adviser for Save the Children said that there

   has been an overemphasis in this conference about drugs.

2. "There is no doubt that the Acme Company will be a difficult and even brutal competitor," company Chairman James Wilson said.

_____

_____

3. "The Justice Department's legal arguments and strategy were flawed," an airline spokesperson said in a statement issued after the Justice Department's announcement.

_____

_____

4. "When you are told you will be freed, you are filled with joy," said Colonel Ortiz.

_____

_____

5. "Without some encouraging news, the markets can't go up," said Johnson Investment's Bill Johnson.

_____

_____

If/Whether Noun Clauses

1. *If/whether* noun clauses begin with *if* or *whether*. Although both have the same meaning, *if* tends to be used in informal contexts and *whether* in more formal situations.

    The politician knows **whether/if she has enough money to run a campaign.**

2. *If* is generally used only when the noun clause is an object of a verb or follows an adjective. It is not used when the noun clause is a subject, a subject complement, or the object of a preposition. *Whether* can always be used.

    I wondered whether/if Alasdair might leave Scotland.

    I thought **about whether** Alasdair might leave Scotland. (object of preposition—*whether* only)

    The question is whether Alasdair might leave Scotland. (subject complement—*whether* only)

IMPORTANT NOTE:

Use statement word order in *if/whether* noun clauses.

I'm not sure **whether he is coming.**

Not: I'm not sure ~~whether is he coming.~~

EXERCISE

11

NOUN CLAUSES WITH *IF/WHETHER*

Use the questions to complete the sentences with noun clauses with if *or* whether. *Make only necessary changes. If both* if *and* whether *are possible, use* if. *The first one is done for you.*

1. Does she understand me?

   I often think about <u>whether she understands me.</u>

2. Could Kevin win the lottery?

   I wonder <u>if / wheter</u>

3. Would the seedlings grow in this soil?

   I'm not sure <u>if / wheter</u>

4. Would Valerie find customers in a new city?

   <u>Wether</u> _____ is the question.

5. Would I find friends who share my interests?

   I often think about _____

EXERCISE

12

EDITING PRACTICE: GRAMMAR FOCUS AND SENTENCE CHECK APPLICATION

Read this paragraph carefully. Find and correct the seven errors in prepositional phrases and noun clauses. The first one is done for you.

An acquaintance of mine is a journalist who needed to take a trip to a rural area to take photographs for a story. He asked me to go along to assist him with carrying equipment, etc. I agreed to the amount of money he offered, but now believe that he owed [owes] me more money. He led me during [to] the most primitive of places. That our living quarters did not even have running water or indoor plumbing I was surprised [me]. For several hours in the day, I carried very heavy lights, cameras, and microphones. After we ate, I went to my room. Exhausted, I went to the bed without even using the well to wash. Later, I heard a noise that woke me up—it was a herd of sheep making noise. I was angry if [that] they are [were] so loud. I am not sure whether is he [he is] going to pay me extra, but I know that I deserve it for having to deal with the hard physical labor, the lack of modern plumbing, and the lack of sleep due to the sheep!

The Writing Process: Practice Writing an Argumentative Essay

Objectives	In Part B, you will:
Prewriting:	search for sources of information to support your argument
Planning:	practice categorizing and synthesizing information from outside sources
	use an outline to organize and sequence ideas for argumentation
Partner Feedback:	review classmates' outlines and analyze feedback
First Draft:	write an argumentative essay
	use "turning an argument on its head" as an introductory technique
Partner Feedback:	review classmates' essays and analyze feedback
Final Draft:	use feedback to write a final draft of your argumentative essay

The Writing Process: Writing Assignment

In the United States there is an ongoing debate about making English the official language of the country. While at first it may be difficult to understand the need for such a law, since more than 90 percent of the inhabitants of the United States have English as their native language, this has become a serious issue for many people on both sides of the debate. Your assignment is to write an essay arguing for one side or the other of this debate. You must justify your position with reasons that support your viewpoint. Follow the steps in the writing process in this section.

Prewriting: Searching for Information to Support Your Argument

IMPORTANT NOTE:

Finding Relevant Sources
of Information

When you search for information for
your essay, follow these guidelines.

▶ Ask the reference librarians how
to find the best sources for your
topic. They can help you learn
how to use electronic materials
as well as find books and journal
articles.

▶ Consider the sources carefully.
Are the authors and publications
credible? Is the article appearing
in a well-respected and peer-
reviewed journal? Again, a reference librarian can assist you in
determining the academic quality
of sources of information.

▶ Keep your notes carefully organized on note cards or typed in a
word processing program.

▶ Make sure that you copy down
all of the information you need
to properly cite your sources,
including the title, author, date
of publication, journal title,
publisher, page numbers, etc.
See Appendix 5, pp. 247–249, as
well as your style manual for
more detailed information.

For an argumentative essay, prewriting usually involves actively seeking information about the issue. Although your teacher will tell you exactly how long or short this essay should be, it will be longer than the usual five- or six-paragraph essays you wrote for the assignments in other units. To develop your argument, you will pull together ideas from a number of different sources, including books, print journal articles, and Internet sources. Your teacher will give you specific guidelines about how many and which kinds of sources you need to include.

Ask a reference librarian at your school to assist you in finding relevant sources for your argumentative essay. Follow the guidelines in the Important Note as well as in Appendix 5, pp. 247–249, to begin gathering information about making English the official language of the United States.

Planning: Synthesizing Information and Using an Outline

Synthesizing Information

A synthesis is a combination of information from two or more sources. When you synthesize, you take information from different sources and blend them smoothly into your essay.

As you read about English only laws or "official English," you will notice that some of the same themes, for example, interference with human rights, reappear in more than one source of information. These themes and ideas will become the reasons you use to develop your argument. What are the themes and ideas that support both views that might be argued? List them.

ENGLISH ONLY LAWS—PRO	ENGLISH ONLY LAWS—CON
_____	_____
_____	_____
_____	_____
_____	_____
_____	_____
_____	_____
_____	_____
_____	_____
_____	_____

Review the information in the chart above. Which ideas do you agree with the most? Which column has more information? Choose one of the two points of view, for or against the issue; in other words, take your stance. Then write a tentative thesis statement that gives your position. Remember that an argumentative thesis statement is distinctive in that it takes a stand. You can change it later if you need to.

Tentative Thesis Statement: _____

_____

Categorizing Details

In your research, you will also notice that some sources of information offer more convincing details and examples than others to support the reasons in favor of or against English-only laws. These details and examples may take several different forms.

▶ A **definition of a key** term may help **explain a point.**

▶ To counter the opposing view, you might **compare and contrast** different approaches or beliefs about English-only laws.

▶ You might show a **cause-effect relationship** between one idea and another.

▶ You may also find **expert or scientific evidence** to support an argument.

To synthesize information from more than one source, you must choose only the best supporting details and methods of showing those details. For example, if you are arguing *against* English-only laws, one reason may be that these laws infringe on the rights of recent immigrants to a fair trial if it is in English and their language skills are not adequate to understand the proceedings. This is how the information might look in a chart.

Reasons	Details	Methods
1. *infringes on rights*	*may not get a fair trial*	*cause-effect*

When you write your essay, you need to make sure that the methods make logical sense for giving the details that will support your argument. For example, you may want to use the definition method in your introduction section to provide background information about English-only laws. Later, you might want to quote an expert on this issue using the expert testimony method to provide supporting details for your argument. Be sure to keep careful notes about which sources you used for each of the details you add to your argument so you can cite your sources properly.

IMPORTANT NOTE:

Remember that you will need to summarize and paraphrase information that you synthesize from sources. For information about these skills, as well as additional information about synthesizing, see Unit 8.

EXERCISE

13

COMPLETING A REASON/DETAIL CHART

*For each **reason** you find in your sources, write at least one **detail** to support it and a **method** of support for each side. Methods may include* definitions, explanations, comparison/contrast, cause/effect, *or* expert testimony. *You may need to add more rows to the charts.*

ENGLISH ONLY LAWS—PRO

Reasons	Details	Methods
1.		
2.		
3.		
4.		

ENGLISH ONLY LAWS—CON

Reasons	Details	Methods
1.		
2.		
3.		
4.		

Using an Outline

Writers usually develop argumentative essays using one of the three methods of organization discussed in Part A. Once you choose a method, you can create an outline that does two things: 1) states and supports your viewpoint and 2) states, acknowledges, and refutes the opposing viewpoint. Organizing the ideas that support your argument lends coherence to your argument, just as using transition expressions do.

Review the three methods of organization that you studied in the Methods of Organization section in Part A (p. 171).

EXERCISE 14

CREATING AN OUTLINE

Use one of the three methods of organization discussed in Part A (pp. x–x) to create an outline to develop your argument either in favor of, or opposed to, a federal English-only law in the United States. Using the information you collected on your research cards and in the chart in Exercise13, organize your outline on a separate piece of paper. You may want to refer to the patterns chart on p. 171 to help you.

Partner Feedback Form 1

Exchange outlines with another student. Read your partner's outline and answer the questions on Partner Feedback Form 1: Unit 7, p. 243, in Appendix 3. Discuss your partner's reactions to your outline. Make notes about any parts you need to change before you write your paper. For more information about giving partner feedback, see Appendix 2, p. 218, Guidelines for Partner Feedback.

First Draft

You are now ready to write the first draft of your essay. Before you begin, review your methods of presenting supporting details chart and any comments from your partner, especially the thesis statement suggestion.

EXERCISE

15

WRITING THE INTRODUCTION

Write an introduction for your essay, using your outline and the feedback you received from your partner. To begin your essay, use "turning an argument on its head" as explained on p. 17, Unit 1, and on this page. Both "Why Adopt a Vegetarian Diet?" on pp. 175–177 and "Coffee: Surprising Benefits from This Herbal Supplement" on pp. 179–180 use this introduction technique. You can use them as models if you want. End your introduction with a well-constructed thesis statement. When you finish, use the checklist to review your work.

IMPORTANT NOTE:

Turning an argument on its head means presenting the opposing view as a starting point. You can use this technique as a hook to generate interest and pull the reader into the essay. After you give the opposing view, you present your own view. Follow it with general ideas and background information about the issue at hand. Then finish your first paragraph with the thesis statement. Here are some tips for using this technique:

▷ Make sure that you can use the opposing view as a starting point in a way that makes sense logically. If you simply state both views, this is not "turning the argument on is head."

▷ Do not go into too much detail for this technique. Use only one or two sentences.

Examples:

Experts agree that developing nations should be encouraged to use modern agricultural techniques, purchasing equipment and seeds from large-scale Western agribusiness companies to bring them into the twenty-first century. However, the very practice of monoculture, or planting only one crop, destroys indigenous people's ability to produce food, shelter, and medicine for themselves.

When trying to finish a term paper or other homework, college students may need to drink caffeinated beverages or even take amphetamines to stay awake. Giving in to the urge to sleep however, by taking a short "cat nap," may in fact be just what you need to refresh yourself and be more productive.

Introduction Checklist

	YES	NO
▶ Did I effectively use an introductory technique such as turning the opposing argument on its head to hook my audience?	☐	☐
▶ Does my introduction include a clear statement of both sides of the issue?	☐	☐
▶ Do I take a stance with my thesis statement? Does my thesis statement provide a clear guide for the reader for the rest of the essay?	☐	☐

What is it? _____

| ▶ Are both views in the debate clear? | ☐ | ☐ |

What are they? _____

EXERCISE

16

WRITING BODY PARAGRAPHS

Look again at your outline and at your introduction. Then complete the body paragraphs. Remember to use correct citation format for your researched information. When you finish, use the checklist to review your work.

Body Paragraph Checklist

	YES	NO
▶ Does each body paragraph treat only one main idea?	☐	☐
▶ Do I successfully follow the method of organization chosen for my outline?	☐	☐
▶ Does each paragraph contain a topic sentence with a clear controlling idea?	☐	☐
▶ Is my viewpoint on this issue clear to the reader?	☐	☐
▶ Do I successfully refute the opposing view?	☐	☐
▶ Are all my methods of presenting supporting details clear and effective? (Check the reasons/details chart in Exercise 13.)	☐	☐
▶ Does each paragraph end with a logical concluding sentence?	☐	☐
▶ Do my body paragraphs all relate to and support the thesis statement of the essay?	☐	☐
▶ Are my body paragraphs arranged in a logical order? That is, do they have coherence?	☐	☐
▶ Are all sentences in my body paragraphs relevant to the topic? That is, do they have unity?	☐	☐

WRITING A CONCLUSION

Review again your outline, introduction, and body. Write a conclusion for your essay. When you finish, use the checklist to review your work.

Conclusion Checklist

	YES	NO
▶ Does my conclusion successfully signal the end of my essay?	☐	☐
▶ Does my conclusion add coherence to the essay by:	☐	☐
a. restating the essay thesis?	☐	☐
b. summarizing or restating my viewpoint?	☐	☐
▶ Does my conclusion:		
a. leave the reader with my final thoughts on the stance I have taken on the issue?	☐	☐
b. make a prediction or suggestion about the topic of the essay?	☐	☐

Partner Feedback Form 2

Exchange essays with another student. Read your partner's essay and answer the questions on Partner Feedback Form 2: Unit 7, p. 245, in Appendix 3. Discuss your partner's reactions to your essay. Make notes about any parts you need to change before you write your second draft. For more information about giving partner feedback, see Appendix 2, p. 218, Guidelines for Partner Feedback.

Final Draft

Carefully revise your essay using all the feedback you have received: partner feedback, review of your outline and essay, instructor comments, and any evaluation you have done yourself. Use the checklist to do a final check of your essay. In addition, try reading your essay aloud. This can help you find awkward-sounding sentences and errors in punctuation. When you finish, add a title to your essay, and neatly type your final draft. See Appendix 4, p. 246, for information about writing titles.

Final Draft Checklist

	YES	NO
▸ Did I include a thesis statement that contains a clear topic and controlling idea?	❏	❏
▸ Which method of organization did I use to develop the argument? _____		
Is the method clear?	❏	❏
▸ Did I argue for only one side of the issue? Did I adequately address opposing views?	❏	❏
▸ Did I synthesize information from different sources well? Did I use correct citation format?	❏	❏
▸ Did I use transition expressions correctly?	❏	❏
▸ Did I use prepositions and noun clauses correctly?	❏	❏
▸ Does each of my body paragraphs have a clear topic sentence?	❏	❏
▸ Does each of my body paragraphs treat one reason or subtopic to support the argument I make?	❏	❏
▸ Does my concluding paragraph successfully signal the end of my essay?	❏	❏
▸ Does my entire essay have unity and coherence?	❏	❏

Additional Writing Assignments from the Academic Disciplines

Beginning with the Prewriting activity on p. 191, use the writing process and write another essay. Choose a topic from the following list.

SUBJECT	*ESSAY WRITING TASK*
Business	Argue for or against moving a manufacturing plant to a less developed country than the United States. What are possible benefits to the host country? What might be harmful?
Science	Argue for or against accepting donations from pharmaceutical companies for scientific research.
Sociology/Political Science	Argue for or against accepting war refugees into more prosperous countries.
Linguistics	Argue for or against bilingual programs in public schools in the United States.

UNIT

8

Blueprints for

PARAPHRASING, SUMMARIZING, AND SYNTHESIZING IN ACADEMIC WRITING

Blueprints for Paraphrasing, Summarizing, and Synthesizing in Academic Writing

Objectives

Analysis:

    Paraphrasing:

    Summarizing:

    Synthesizing:

Practice:

In Unit 8, you will:

learn the difference between quoting and paraphrasing

study paraphrasing examples

learn summarizing guidelines

study example summaries

learn the steps for synthesizing

study synthesis examples

practice paraphrasing and summarizing information

practice synthesizing information while writing a cause/effect essay

IMPORTANT NOTE:

Plagiarism is passing off someone else's writing and ideas as your own—like stealing what belongs to someone else. It is a serious issue in academic circles. If you turn in an assignment that you were supposed to write but did not write, you can suffer terrible consequences such as academic probation or even expulsion from a college or university.

Plagiarism is not always intentional. Sometimes you find information from a book, an article, or a web site that you believe is an excellent fact or support for your essay. However, if you do not put quotations around the exact words or paraphrase the information, you are in effect stealing the academic property of the original writer. In order to use source materials correctly and avoid plagiarism, learn the skills of paraphrasing, summarizing, and synthesizing and then apply correct documentation format. (See Appendix 5 for information about documenting sources.)

What Are Paraphrasing, Summarizing, and Synthesizing?

In academic writing, you will often have to write about something you have read. Therefore, it is important to learn how to **paraphrase** (use different language to say the same thing), **summarize** (express the same idea in a smaller number of words), and **synthesize** (combine information from two or more sources) to answer a specific question of interest.

Study the diagram on the next page. It shows how you may paraphrase a source, summarize a source, and then use these skills to synthesize information from two or more sources into your original writing.

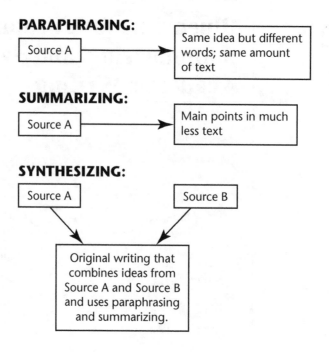

PARAPHRASING:

Source A → Same idea but different words; same amount of text

SUMMARIZING:

Source A → Main points in much less text

SYNTHESIZING:

Source A   Source B

Original writing that combines ideas from Source A and Source B and uses paraphrasing and summarizing.

Paraphrasing

When you write an essay, you use your original ideas and information you have learned through experience. In addition, you often use information from print and electronic sources such as books, web sites, magazines, and newspapers. You can use such source information in two ways, and both ways show that you borrowed this information. The first way is to put *quotation marks* around the exact words.

Example:

According to a study in the *The Lancet,* "Lipid-lowering agents are known to reduce long-term mortality in patients with stable coronary disease or significant risk factors. Might they also be effective in reducing short-term mortality after acute coronary syndromes? An observational study suggests they are."

A second way of using information that is not yours is to **paraphrase,** or to re-state, another writer's words and ideas in your own words.

Paraphrase Example:

A recent study in *The Lancet* indicates that lipid-lowering drugs may increase short-term survival rates after acute coronary syndromes in the same way that they increase long-term survival rates for patients with stable coronary disease or with significant risk factors.

CAREFUL! In both of these examples, you need to avoid plagiarism and use parenthetical documentation to tell where you found the original material. (See Appendix 5 for information about documenting sources.)

IMPORTANT NOTE:

How do you introduce information from an outside source? One way is to use the phrase *According to* followed by the author's name or the name of the book.

Example: **According to** a report in the *New England Journal of Medicine,* . . . (your paraphrase)

Another way is to use the name of the source with a verb, such as *state, say, argue, believe, reveal, conclude, report,* or *suggest,* that indicates a sharing of the information.

Example: The *New England Journal of Medicine* **reported that** . . . (your paraphrase)

A good paraphrase conveys the same ideas and information as the original writing, but in different words. As the example above shows, the length of the paraphrase may be similar to the original, but the grammar and vocabulary are usually not the same. Key vocabulary, which may be technical, is often the same because there may not be another way to state it.

In English, the verbs that name a source (for example, *state, say, argue, believe, reveal, conclude, report,* and *suggest*) are sometimes used in the present tense rather than the past tense; however, both tenses have the same meaning.

Examples:

The New York Times **states** (stated) that tourism in New York City is at an all-time high.

The investigator **believes** (believed) that the ship's captain is responsible for the accident.

Examples of Paraphrasing

Paraphrasing is an extremely important skill for all academic writers. Study these examples of good and bad paraphrasing.

Original (13 words)	*Main idea to keep:*
Selling a product successfully in another country often requires changes in the product.	Companies must change their products to succeed in another country

Good paraphrase (15 words)	
The most successful exporting companies have succeeded because they made important changes in their products.	1. It keeps the idea that change is necessary. 2. Grammar is different (*subject:* exporting companies; *verb:* have succeeded; *dependent clause:* because they made important changes in their products). 3. Vocabulary is different (successful exporting companies, have succeeded because, important). 4. Length is similar to original.

Poor paraphrase (14 words)

To sell a product <u>successfully</u> in another country, you need to change the product.

Main idea to keep:

1. The ideas are the same, but the wording is too similar (successfully, in another country). *In fact, it is almost exactly the same. (Reread the original above.) This is plagiarism!*

2. Though the length is similar to the original, only minor changes were made (Selling = To sell; often requires = you need to)

EXERCISE 1

PARAPHRASING: MULTIPLE CHOICE

*Read the original sentence. Then read the three possible paraphrases. Mark one **B** (Best), one **TS** (Too Similar), and one **D** (Different—or wrong—information).*

SOURCE 1

Pages 93–96

UNIT 4—BLUEPRINT COMPARISON/CONTRAST ESSAY 1: "EXAMINING THE POPULARITY OF JULIA ROBERTS' CHARACTERS"

1. *Despite the differences in these characters, perhaps it is their similarities that have attracted so many millions of moviegoers to **Pretty Woman** and **Erin Brockovich**.*

   B ✓ a. The main characters played by Julia Roberts in both *Pretty Woman* and *Erin Brockovich* were different yet possibly alike enough to draw many film patrons.

   D b. Julia Roberts played Erin Brockovich and Vivian Ward, who were similar characters in two movies.

   TS c. Despite the distinction between these characters, one can draw a parallel that has attracted so many millions of moviegoers to *Pretty Woman* and *Erin Brockovich*.

SOURCE 2

Pages 66–68

UNIT 3—BLUEPRINT PROCESS ESSAY 1: "BABY TALK"

2. *States of hunger, pain, or discomfort that cause crying and fussing are common at this stage.*

   B ✓ a. Babies normally cry and protest during this phase because they hurt in some way or are hungry.

   TS b. States of hunger or discomfort that cause crying and fussing are frequent at this stage.

   D c. States of hunger, pain, or discomfort that cause crying and protest are uncommon at this stage.

(continued)

(continued)

SOURCE 3

Pages 124–125

UNIT 5—BLUEPRINT CAUSE/EFFECT ESSAY 1:
"MARKETING HEALTH AND FITNESS"

3. *Adolescents cannot escape the constant barrage of ads on television and radio and in magazines and newspapers. While some teenagers take this new-found knowledge and begin eating more appropriate foods and exercising regularly, others become obsessed with weight loss.*

_Is_ a. There is no escape for adolescents from the constant <u>onslaught</u> of ads on television and radio and in magazines and newspapers. Although some take this new knowledge and begin eating better foods and exercising regularly, others become fixated on weight loss.

_B_ b. Even though there are many opportunities for teenagers to learn about proper diet and exercise, many disregard this information and focus solely on losing weight.

_D_ c. Advertisements are constantly telling adolescents to be supermodel-thin; as a result, many teenagers starve themselves to death.

EXERCISE 2

PARAPHRASING PRACTICE: WRITE YOUR OWN

Read these original sentences and passages from Blueprint essays in other units. Circle what you consider to be the most important ideas. Then write your own paraphrase of the sentence or passage.

SOURCE 1

Pages 10–11

UNIT 1—"JOB SKILLS"

1. One way in which career counselors try to match people with their ideal jobs is according to the broadly-defined categories of skills that the jobs require.

Your paraphrase: A form that career Counselors want to conect people with their dream jobs, is getting an slactitics of the abilities that they need to work.

SOURCE 1

Pages 10–11

UNIT 1—"JOB SKILLS"

2. In fact, today's medical schools are giving almost as much weight to the interpersonal skills of their applicants as they do to their mental skills when evaluating these candidates for acceptance into their training programs.

Your paraphrase: _____

_____

(continued)

(continued)

SOURCE **2**
Pages 37–39

UNIT 2—"TEN THOUSAND TEAS"

3. The fresh tea leaves that are used for green tea are quickly steamed to halt bacterial and enzyme action common in fermentation.

stop (written under "halt")

Your paraphrase: The natural tea which is used to green tea are faster evaporeted to stop microbe and enzyme current procediment in fermentation.

UNIT 2—"TEN THOUSAND TEAS"

SOURCE **2**
Pages 37–39

4. These two processes are repeated until the leaves become almost transparent and start to yellow or redden along the edges, which is a sign of the beginnings of fermentation.

Your paraphrase: _____

_____

SOURCE **3**
Pages 97–98

UNIT 4—BLUEPRINT COMPARISON/CONTRAST ESSAY 2— "TWO KINDS OF ENGLISH"

5. Pronunciation is perhaps the first difference that people notice between American and British English. Some individual sounds are consistently different. For example, PoTAYto in American English comes out as poTAHto in British English. WateR in American English is pronounced as wateH in British English. TUna in American English comes out as TYUna in British English. Furthermore, certain whole words are pronounced quite differently. *Schedule* is pronounced with a "k" sound in American English but with a "sh" sound, as *shedule,* in British English. The stress in the word *aluminum* in American English is on the second syllable, so it is pronounced aLUminum by Americans. Stress in this same word in British English is on the third syllable, so British English speakers pronounce it aluMInum. These pronunciation differences, though noticeable, do not impede real communication. In addition, neither American English nor British English has a better pronunciation than the other; they are simply different.

Your paraphrase: _____

_____

_____

_____

_____

_____

_____

(continued)

Pages 175–177

(continued)

UNIT 7—BLUEPRINT ARGUMENTATIVE ESSAY 1—
"WHY ADOPT A VEGETARIAN DIET?"

6. One reason for becoming vegetarian is to prevent cruelty to animals. Animals, like humans, feel pain, stress, and fear. People cannot morally justify the pain and suffering of animals that are killed for food when adequate nutrition can be found in plant foods. Not only do animals experience these physical sensations when they are needlessly slaughtered for human consumption, but they are often treated cruelly prior to slaughter. Veal calves, for example, are forced to live in extremely small cages no longer than their bodies so they cannot move and create unwanted muscle. They are then killed when they are just twelve to sixteen weeks old so that their weak, immature muscles will produce soft meat.

Your paraphrase: People that don't want eat meat anymore are trying to avoid the murder of animals. Animals are humans too and they can feel when others hurt them, be afraid and be stressful. Humans don't have a true reason to hurt and

Summarizing

Remember that quoting and paraphrasing are techniques you can use to include information from another source in your writing. Another way to include information from another source is by **summarizing** it. A summary is a shortened version, in your own words, of someone else's ideas. These ideas may come from an article, a book, or a lecture. In college courses, knowing how to write summaries can be useful. For example, you may be asked to answer a test question with a short paragraph that summarizes the key points in your lecture notes. Before you can write a research paper, you will need to summarize the main ideas in your sources of information. When you summarize, you do not include all the information from the source. Instead, you use only the most important parts.

Summarizing involves not only writing but also reading and critical thinking. To summarize, you should do the following.

GUIDELINES FOR SUMMARIZING

1. Read the source material and understand it well.

2. Decide which parts of the source material are the most important.

3. Put the important parts in the same order they appear in the original.

4. Paraphrase (see pp. 202–207)— use different grammar and vocabulary. **You must write information in your own words.**

5. If the original states a point and then gives multiple examples, include a general statement with just one example.

6. Use verbs that indicate that you are summarizing information from a source (and not from your own head) such as *suggest, report, argue, tell, say, ask, question,* and *conclude.*

Remember that a summary is always shorter than the original writing. A ten-page article might become a few paragraphs in a summary. A two-hundred page book might become an essay.

Examples of Summarizing

Summarizing is a very important skill for a good writer. It is especially important when you are taking information from long sources. Study these examples of good and poor summarizing.

Original (190 words)

Selling a product successfully in another country often requires changes in the original product. Domino's Pizza offers mayonnaise and potato pizza in Tokyo and pickled ginger pizza in India. Heinz varies its ketchup recipe to satisfy the needs of specific markets. In Belgium and Holland, for example, the ketchup is not as sweet as it is in the United States. When Haagen-Dazs served up one of its most popular American flavors, Chocolate Chip Cookie Dough, to British customers, they left it sitting in supermarket freezers. What the premium ice-cream maker learned is that chocolate chip cookies are not popular in Great Britain, and children do not have a history of snatching raw dough from the bowl. For this reason, the company had to develop flavors that would sell in

Main ideas to keep:
1. Companies must change their products to succeed.
2. Examples of companies that did this: Domino's, Heinz, Haagen-Dazs, Frito-Lay.

Great Britain. Because dairy products are not part of Chinese diets, Frito-Lay took the cheese out of Chee-tos in China. Instead, the company sells Seafood Chee-tos. Without a doubt, these products were so successful in these foreign lands only because the company realized that it was wise to do market research and make fundamental changes in the products.

Main ideas to keep:

Good Summary (31 words):

Companies must adapt their products if they want to do well in foreign markets. Many well-known companies, including Domino's, Heinz, Haagen-Daz, and Frito-Lay, have altered their products and proved this point.

1. It covers the main ideas.
2. It is a true summary, not an exact repeat of the specific examples.
3. It includes some new grammar, for example:
   Original text: often requires changes
   Summary: modal is used: "companies **must** adapt"

4. It includes some new vocabulary, for example:
   Original text: Specific country names
   Summary: "many well-known companies"

Poor Summary (174 words)

Changes in a product are important if a company wants to sell it successfully in another country. For example, Domino's Pizza offers mayonnaise and potato pizza in Tokyo and pickled ginger pizza in India. In addition, Heinz has changed its ketchup recipe to satisfy the needs of specific markets. In Belgium and Holland the ketchup is less sweet. When Haagen-Dazs served up one of its most popular American flavors, Chocolate Chip Cookie Dough, to British customers, the British customers left it sitting in supermarket freezers. The luxury ice-cream maker learned that

1. It is almost as long as the original and, therefore, not really a summary.
2. It includes almost the same vocabulary, for example:
   Original text: the premium ice-cream maker
   Summary: the luxury ice-cream maker (This is plagiarism!)

chocolate chip cookies are not popular in Great Britain, and children do not take uncooked dough from the bowl. For this reason, the company developed flavors to sell in Great Britain. Since dairy products are not usually eaten in China, Frito-Lay removed the cheese from Chee-tos in China. In its place, the company has Seafood Chee-tos. Certainly, these items were so successful in these countries only because the company was smart enough to do market research and implement fundamental changes in the products.

Main idea to keep:

3. It includes almost the same grammar, for example:
Original text: For this reason, the company had to develop flavors that would sell in Great Britain.
Summary: For this reason, the company developed flavors to sell in Great Britain.
(This is plagiarism!)

SUMMARIZING: IDENTIFYING THE MOST IMPORTANT IDEAS

Reread Blueprint Process Essay 2 (Unit 3, pp. 70–71) "Exercise for Everyone." Choose at least four important facts and ideas from the essay. Then paraphrase each fact or idea in note form, using phrases, not complete sentences.

1. _____

_____

2. _____

_____

3. _____

_____

4. _____

_____

| EXERCISE | # Summarizing: Putting It in Your Own Words |

4

Using your ideas from Exercise 3, write five to seven sentences that summarize the original message of "Exercise for Everyone."

_____

_____

_____

_____

_____

_____

Synthesizing

A synthesis is a combination of information from two or more sources. When you synthesize, you take information from different sources and blend them smoothly into your paragraph.

BASIC STEPS FOR SYNTHESIZING

1. Read the material from all the sources.

2. Choose the important ideas from each source. For this task, you must analyze the information. Ask yourself, "What is the author's purpose for writing this information?" Then decide which pieces of information are most important in accomplishing what the author intends. In synthesizing, it is always necessary to use only the important, relevant information.

3. Group together the ideas that are connected and that support each other.

4. Combine the ideas in each group into sentences, using your paraphrasing skills.

5. Organize the sentences into logical paragraphs and combine them into one continuous piece of writing. Be sure to include an introduction, well-constructed body paragraphs, and a conclusion. Do not forget to include any original ideas you have, too.

6. Check your work for accuracy and smoothness. Add transition words where they are needed.

Synthesis Examples

Synthesis is an important skill for academic writers who often use more than one source when writing papers. Study these examples of good and poor synthesizing.

Source A (81 words)

Switzerland is a great example of linguistic diversity because there are three different national languages. People in the central and northern areas speak German. People in the western area speak French. People in the southeastern area of the country speak Italian. Most Swiss can speak more than one language. One interesting fact is that the name of the country on its coins and stamps is not in any of these languages. Instead, "Helvetia," the Latin name for this country, is used.
Claudio Acevedo, Argentina

Main ideas to keep:
1. *Geographical areas of Switzerland speak different languages.*
2. *Central and northern regions = German*
3. *Western part = French; southeastern region = Italian*
4. *The Latin name for Switzerland is used as well!!*

Source B (68 words)

You might think that most people in Switzerland speak the same language because it is a rather small country. However, you would be wrong. Yes, the country is tiny, but there are four national languages. German is spoken by more people than any other language. The second most commonly spoken language is French, and Italian is third. A very small percentage of the people speak Romansch.
Najmuddin bin Faisal, Malaysia

1. *Most Swiss speak German, then French, then Italian, and finally a few people in Switzerland speak Romansch.*

Good synthesis (110 words)

Although Switzerland is a small country, several languages are spoken there. In fact, this tiny country has four national languages. The most commonly spoken language is German, which is used in the central and northern regions. The second most widely spoken language is French, which is used in the western area of the country. The third most-commonly used language is Italian, which is spoken in the southeastern area of Switzerland. A fourth language, Romansch, is spoken by only a very small percentage of the population. Ironically, the name for Switzerland on Swiss currency is not in any of these languages. Instead, *Helvetia*, the Latin term for this country, is used.

Main ideas to keep:

1. *It has ideas from both sources (for example, Source A:* German is spoken in central and northern regions; *Source B:* the most common language is German)
2. *The ideas are woven together.* (The most commonly spoken language is German, which is used in the central and northern regions.)
3. *The sequence of the material is logical. (first, second, third, fourth most common languages)*

Poor synthesis (88 words)

Switzerland is tiny, but there are four national languages. The languages in order of usage are: German, French, Italian, and Romansch. Portuguese and Greek are not spoken in this country. People in the western area speak French. People in the southeastern area of the country speak Italian. People in the central and northern areas speak German. One interesting fact is that the name of the country on its coins and stamps is not in any of these languages. Instead, *Helvetia*, the Latin name for this country, is used.

1. *The ideas are not woven together very well. It is easy to see where one source ends and another begins. Source 2 information ends after* The languages in order of usage are: German, French, Italian, and Romansch. *Source 1 information takes up the rest of the paragraph.*
2. *The third sentence is an unrelated idea about Portuguese and Greek that is not from either source.*
3. *The sequence of the languages by geographical areas is illogical because it does not match the list of languages given at the beginning of the paragraph.*

Synthesizing: Essay Question Practice

Imagine that you are a student in a sociology class. In an essay of five to eight paragraphs, write your answer to the essay question below using a word processing computer program. In your essay, synthesize information from a variety of sources.

SOCIOLOGY EXAM QUESTION

In a cause/effect essay, discuss the relationship between globalization and human rights. Briefly define globalization and human rights. Then explain how globalization has impacted human rights around the world.

Be sure to review the complete set of steps for process writing in the Part B sections of the previous units, including Prewriting, Planning, First Draft, Partner Feedback, and Final Draft. Pay attention especially to Unit 5 for information on cause/effect essays (See Unit 5, pp. 118–143.)

The following diagram will remind you of the synthesizing process. Although the diagram shows only two sources of information, ask your teacher how many sources you should use.

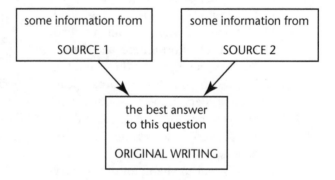

To develop your essay, follow these Basic Steps for Synthesizing.

Step 1: Read the material—Pull together ideas about globalization and human rights from a number of different sources, including books, print journal articles, and Internet sources. Ask a reference librarian at your school to assist you in finding relevant sources for your essay. **Remember to write down all the information you need about the sources to properly give credit.** (See Appendix 5, Finding and Documenting Information from Sources on pp. 247–250.)

Source 1: _____

_____

Source 2: _____

_____

Source 3: _____

_____

Step 2: Choose the important ideas from each source—As you read about your topic in the sources, you will notice that some of the same themes reappear in more than one source of information. Decide which are the most important and relevant pieces of information and list them below.

Source 1: _____

_____

_____

_____

Source 2: _____

_____

_____

_____

Source 3: _____

_____

_____

_____

Step 3: Group together the ideas that are connected and that support each other—Place the ideas you listed in Step 2 into categories that fit together. Your list of ideas for each group may be longer or shorter than the lines provided.

Group 1 Main Idea _____

Related Idea _____

Related Idea _____

Related Idea _____

Related Idea _____

Group 2 Main Idea _____

Related Idea _____

Related Idea _____

Related Idea _____

Related Idea _____

Group 3 Main Idea _____

Related Idea _____

Related Idea _____

Related Idea _____

Related Idea _____

Group 4 Main Idea _____

Related Idea _____

Related Idea _____

Related Idea _____

Related Idea _____

Step 4: Combine the ideas in each group into sentences, using your paraphrasing skills—Using a word processing program, type the ideas you categorized in Step 3, combining the ideas in each of the groups into sentences.

Step 5: Organize the sentences into logical paragraphs and combine them into one continuous piece of writing, using transition expressions. Be sure to include an introduction, well-constructed body paragraphs, and a conclusion. Do not forget to include any original ideas you have, too—Revise and develop the sentences you created, organizing them coherently into an essay.

Step 6: Check your work for accuracy and smoothness. Add transition words where they are needed—Check your essay again for any revisions needed, and then turn it in to your teacher.

Finding and Documenting Information from Sources

Finding Information from Different Sources

A research paper differs in at least two ways from the kinds of essays you have learned how to write in the early units of this book.

First, the research paper requires you to use information from more than one source of ideas. Also, as indicated in Unit 7, research papers are longer than an essay of five to seven paragraphs. To adequately develop your ideas about a topic, you must find out as much about it as you can to truly formulate your own thinking about it. You must take the responsibility for finding ideas beyond those given to you by your teacher in articles, handouts, or textbooks. You can find books, journal articles, and electronic materials at your college library.

Since the early 1990s, many libraries have begun to make electronic materials available. Students can now find electronic versions of print journals and newspapers. In addition to taking up less physical space in the library, these electronic materials are easier than print to search and find something specific.

In-Text Citations

When you include information from an original source in your final essay, you must cite this source in your text. There are several styles for citing material. One of the most common is to list the author of the material and the publication date.

In the examples that follow, note how the student writer uses part of Zumdahl's information in his work. Pay attention to the wording of the original source, the wording of the student writing, and the manner in which the information is cited.

SOURCE 1

ORIGINAL SOURCE

Although some chemical industries have been culprits in the past for fouling the earth's environment, that situation is rapidly changing. In fact, a quiet revolution is sweeping through chemistry from academic labs to Fortune 500 companies. Chemistry is going green. *Green chemistry* means minimizing hazardous wastes, substituting water and other environmentally friendlier substances for traditional organic solvents, and manufacturing productions out of recyclable materials.

From S. Zumdahl, *Introductory Chemistry*, (Boston: Houghton Mifflin, 2000).

Possible citation: According to Zumdahl (2000), green chemistry has three basic components.

Possible Citation: Zumdahl (2000) discusses the quiet revolution that is taking place within the chemistry world.

Student writing using the original source:

Most people would regard chemistry as a very traditional branch of science, but there are new hybrids of this traditional science. Green chemistry is a good example of a new version of a traditional field of study. <u>According to Zumdahl (2000), green chemistry has three basic components, including creating fewer dangerous wastes, using water as a solvent, and working with schools to include tolerance.</u> Because it is so new, green chemistry has yet to prove itself to be a true advancement over traditional chemistry. However, green chemistry seems to have a great deal of potential.

Common ways for writing the citation include:

▸ <u>According to</u> Zumdahl, this medicine has serious problems . . .

▸ Zumdahl <u>found</u> that this medicine had serious problems . . .

▸ Zumdahl <u>reported</u> that this medicine had serious problems . . .

    ▸ A report by Zumdahl <u>showed</u> that this medicine had serious problems . . .

    ▸ Zumdahl <u>concluded</u> that this medicine had serious problems . . .

    ▸ <u>Based on</u> Zumdahl's findings, we may conclude that . . .

    ▸ <u>Based on</u> Zumdahl's results, it may be concluded that . . .

    ▸ <u>Because of</u> Zumdahl's results, this medicine is no longer used . . .

    ▸ <u>From</u> Zumdahl's work, we know that this medicine has serious problems . . .

    ▸ Zumdahl <u>proved</u> that this medicine has serious problems . . .

IMPORTANT NOTE:

If your field has a special guide for citations, follow the rules or guidelines in that guide. Examples of special guides for citations include MLA (Modern Language Association), APA (American Psychological Association), and *The Chicago Manual of Style* (University of Chicago Press). In these guides, you will find examples for citing sources in the body of your essay; you will also find information about how to create lists of these sources at the end of your essay or research paper.

Reference Lists (Bibliographies)

In addition to citing sources, you will need to create a bibliography for these sources at the end of your paper. There are several styles for doing this. Here are some examples:

1. American Psychological Association (APA) Style—used for psychology, education and other social sciences
   a. For a book—Zinn, Howard. (1980). *A People's History of the United States.* New York: HarperCollins.
   b. For a journal article—St. Denis, V. (2000). Indigenous Peoples, Globalization, and Education: Making Connections. *Alberta Journal of Educational Research, 46*(1), 36–48.

2. Modern Language Association (MLA) Style—used for literature, arts and humanities
   a. For a book— Zinn, Howard. A People's History of the United States. New York: HarperCollins, 1980.
   b. For a journal article—St. Denis, Verna. "Indigenous Peoples, Globalization, and Education: Making Connections." Alberta Journal of Educational Research 46.1 (2000) 36–48.

3. Style Presented in *The Chicago Manual of Style*—used for most books, magazines, and newspapers of a journalistic nature.
   a. For a book—Zinn, Howard. 1980. *A People's History of the United States.* New York: HarperCollins.
   b. For a journal article—St. Denis, Verna. 2000. Indigenous Peoples, Globalization, and Education: Making Connection. *Alberta Journal of Educational Research* 46 (1): 36–48.

You should check with your teacher for the style he or she prefers that you use. In addition, the examples presented above illustrate only two common types of sources. For more information on how to include other types of sources (for example, sources written by more than one author, Web sources, etc), consult a publication style manual recommended by your teacher.

IMPORTANT NOTE:

Searching the Internet: The best way to find scholarly sources of information is through your college library. Doing a random Internet search for information for a research paper is not the best way to find credible, academic sources of information. However, you may want to search the Internet for information like the e-mail address of a professor who wrote an article you like, for example.

There are two primary ways to search for information on the Internet. One way is to use a search engine, like Google. The other way is to use a web directory like Yahoo. A good way to understand the difference between the two is to think of a search engine like an index in a book. It contains specific information about the entire book. A web directory is like the table of contents. It contains the broad categories that make up the chapters of the book. You would use a search engine when you are looking for something very specific, whereas you would use a web directory when you are looking for broader ideas.

CPSIA information can be obtained
at www.ICGtesting.com
Printed in the USA
FFHW01n0408290718
47567815-51039FF